The Great
Steam Trains
America's Great Smoking Iron Horses

Fredric Winkowski   Charles Fulkerson Jr

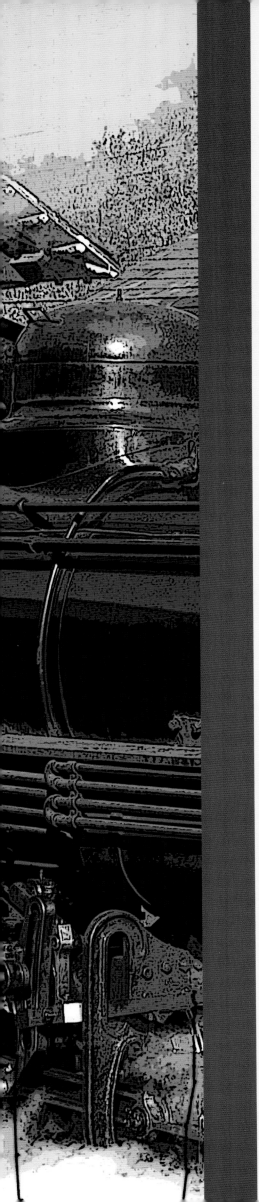
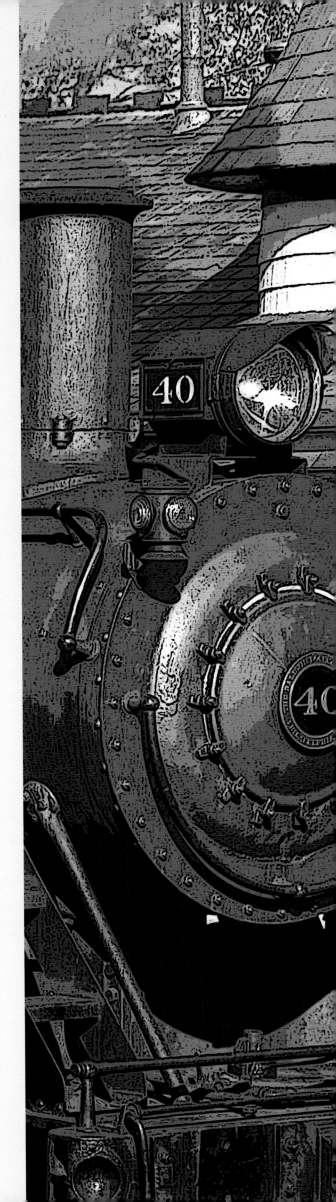

The Great
Steam
Trains

*America's Great Smoking
Iron Horses*

Fredric Winkowski
Charles Fulkerson Jr.

additional photography by

Frank D. Sullivan

paintings by

Charles Fulkerson Jr.

p

This is a Parragon Publishing Book
First published in 2006
Conceived and produced by Glitterati Incorporated/www.glitteratiincorporated.com

Parragon Publishing
Queen Street House
4 Queen Street
Bath BA1 1HE, UK

ISBN 1-40547-596-X

Dedication:
To all of those who love and are inspired by history.
        --FW

To train-watchers; especially Charles II and the late Charles, Sr.
        --CF

Contents

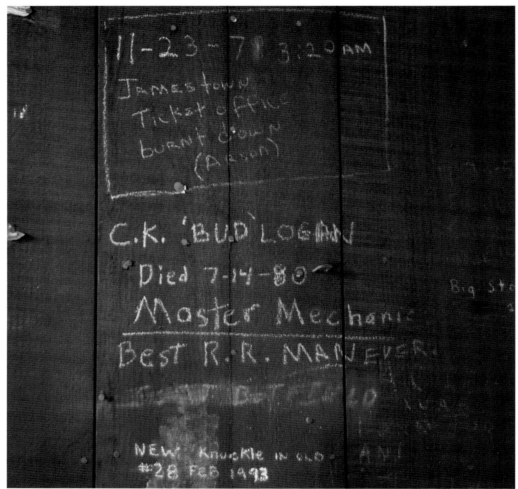

Photographed on a shop wall at Railtown 1897, California State Historic Park, Jamestown, CA

*For 180 years, railroaders have shared danger
and hardship. This old chalk epitaph in
Jamestown, California, attests to the family-like
bonds between railroaders.*

Preface

Machines We Love

We're both old enough to have been small boys when the biggest and loudest thing in our young lives was the steam engine. As with most young boys in the 1940s, we were enthralled by the locomotive—the blasting steam and belching smoke…the panting din…the way it shook the ground when we were brave enough to climb off our fathers' shoulders.

For millions of Americans in the early 20th century, trains ran in the family. Chuck's father worked summers as a surveyor on the Rock Island Railroad before graduating from MIT—in the days when the marvel of mechanical engineering was still the steam locomotive. A great-uncle worked as a Milwaukee Road engineer between Kansas City and Chillicothe, Missouri. Chuck's wife had a great uncle who was an engineer on the Chicago & Northwestern Railway. Eventually Chuck became a writer and journalist, and this is his second book.

For Fred, all things that moved were fascinating. As a youngster he filled his sketchpads with drawings of planes, trains and cars. And now as a photographer, Fred finds great beauty in the faded elegance of old train cars, the patina of stained iron and steel, the great muscle visible in a machine that exposes its complex workings so openly. Pursuing this beauty has led to a dozen books devoted to vintage transportation, with this being his third book on trains.

Both of us, whether wearing the hats of writer or painter, graphic designer or photographer, are still entranced by the spell of railroading. The track-side aroma of tar, oil, coal and iron are enticing perfumes. And few things are more exciting to us than hiking over and under hazardous trestles to catch sight of the spinning wheels and flashing rods of a living, exhaling, speeding locomotive. The fascination with all mechanical, moving things has endured.

This book is the distillation of the experience of several generations of railroading families, two creative lifetimes and one great enthusiasm. For us, it has been an honor to have the opportunity to celebrate the steam locomotive in these pages—and to bond with three generations of railroad lovers. We hope our enthusiasm will be contagious, especially to the next generation of rail fans.

Charles Fulkerson Jr.
Fredric Winkowski

July 2006

Introduction

The Steam Age

Swift as the wind and loud as thunder, the steam train took America by storm, driving the nation into the modern age and turning the United States into an industrial colossus.

With the stroke of a piston, time and distance were transformed. Travel was no longer measured in weeks and months, but in minutes and hours.

The clock, and time itself, was set by steam. Speeding steam trains and tight schedules required split-second time keeping—leading directly to synchronized watches and national time zones. Railroad time was on time!

Like the Iron Age and the ancient eras of early man, the Steam Age heralded profound change. The train became as much a part of daily life as the horse before it, and the automobile afterwards. Over 160,000 steam locomotives ruled the rails for well over a century. New industries sprang up to serve the ever-expanding steam railroads. Millions of Americans found jobs building, running and maintaining the magnificent steam locomotives and their gleaming rails.

The subject of song, story and legend, the steam locomotive was beloved, its exploits celebrated. With his hand on the throttle of immense power and responsibility, the locomotive engineer was handsomely paid, highly respected and idolized by schoolboys everywhere.

But steam's dominance ended almost overnight. In little more than a decade nearly all the steam locomotives vanished. Even the newest and most powerful dropped their fires, towed into scrap-yard oblivion. Their undoing was the diesel-electric engine, an ultra-efficient machine with the comparative romance and intrigue of a delivery truck.

Today, thanks to luck and foresight, a few hundred steam locomotives are preserved. Some still operate, a moving tribute to the glory of steam.

This is the story in remarkable pictures and words of the heroic steam train, its legacy and the proud survivors of one of the greatest inventions of all time.

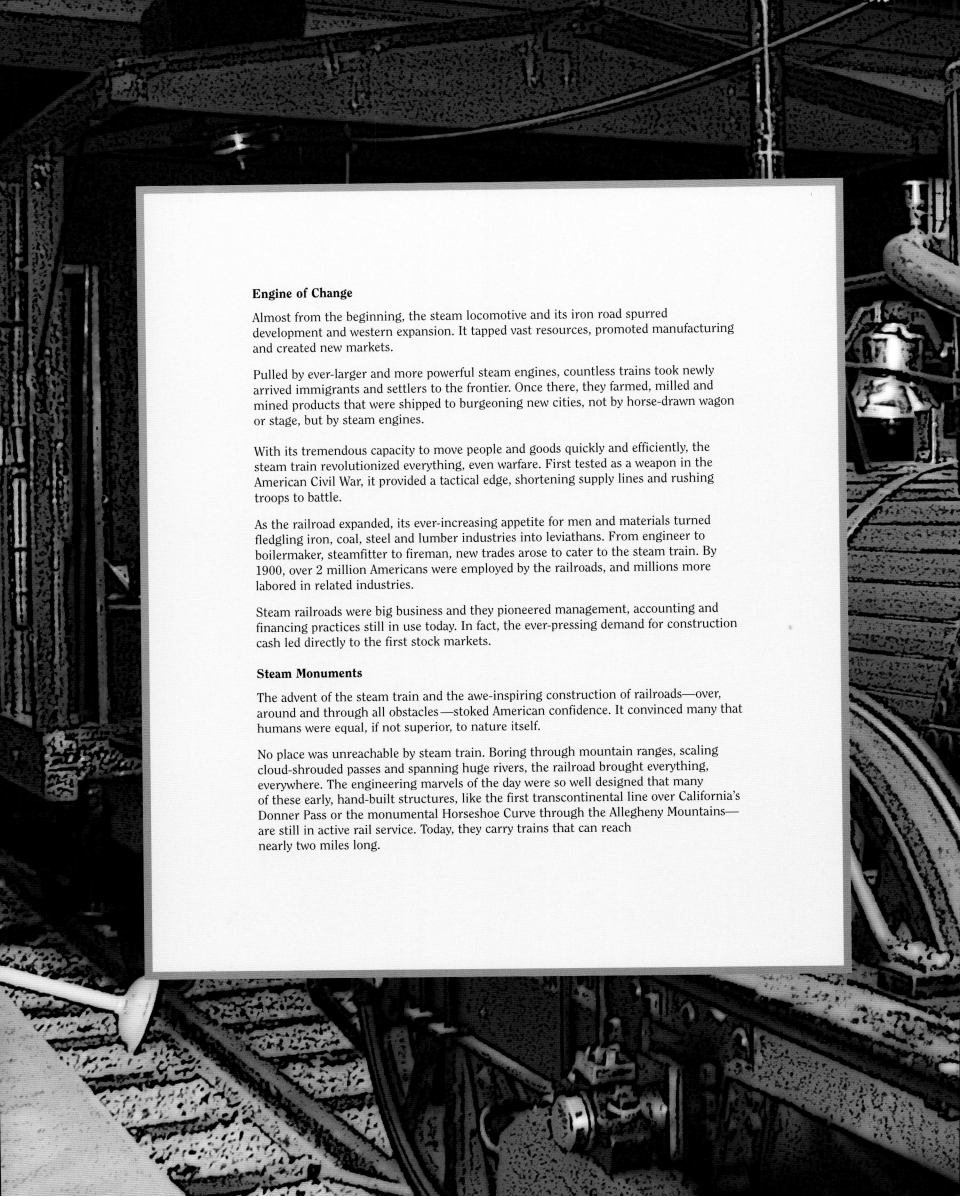

Engine of Change

Almost from the beginning, the steam locomotive and its iron road spurred development and western expansion. It tapped vast resources, promoted manufacturing and created new markets.

Pulled by ever-larger and more powerful steam engines, countless trains took newly arrived immigrants and settlers to the frontier. Once there, they farmed, milled and mined products that were shipped to burgeoning new cities, not by horse-drawn wagon or stage, but by steam engines.

With its tremendous capacity to move people and goods quickly and efficiently, the steam train revolutionized everything, even warfare. First tested as a weapon in the American Civil War, it provided a tactical edge, shortening supply lines and rushing troops to battle.

As the railroad expanded, its ever-increasing appetite for men and materials turned fledgling iron, coal, steel and lumber industries into leviathans. From engineer to boilermaker, steamfitter to fireman, new trades arose to cater to the steam train. By 1900, over 2 million Americans were employed by the railroads, and millions more labored in related industries.

Steam railroads were big business and they pioneered management, accounting and financing practices still in use today. In fact, the ever-pressing demand for construction cash led directly to the first stock markets.

Steam Monuments

The advent of the steam train and the awe-inspiring construction of railroads—over, around and through all obstacles—stoked American confidence. It convinced many that humans were equal, if not superior, to nature itself.

No place was unreachable by steam train. Boring through mountain ranges, scaling cloud-shrouded passes and spanning huge rivers, the railroad brought everything, everywhere. The engineering marvels of the day were so well designed that many of these early, hand-built structures, like the first transcontinental line over California's Donner Pass or the monumental Horseshoe Curve through the Allegheny Mountains— are still in active rail service. Today, they carry trains that can reach nearly two miles long.

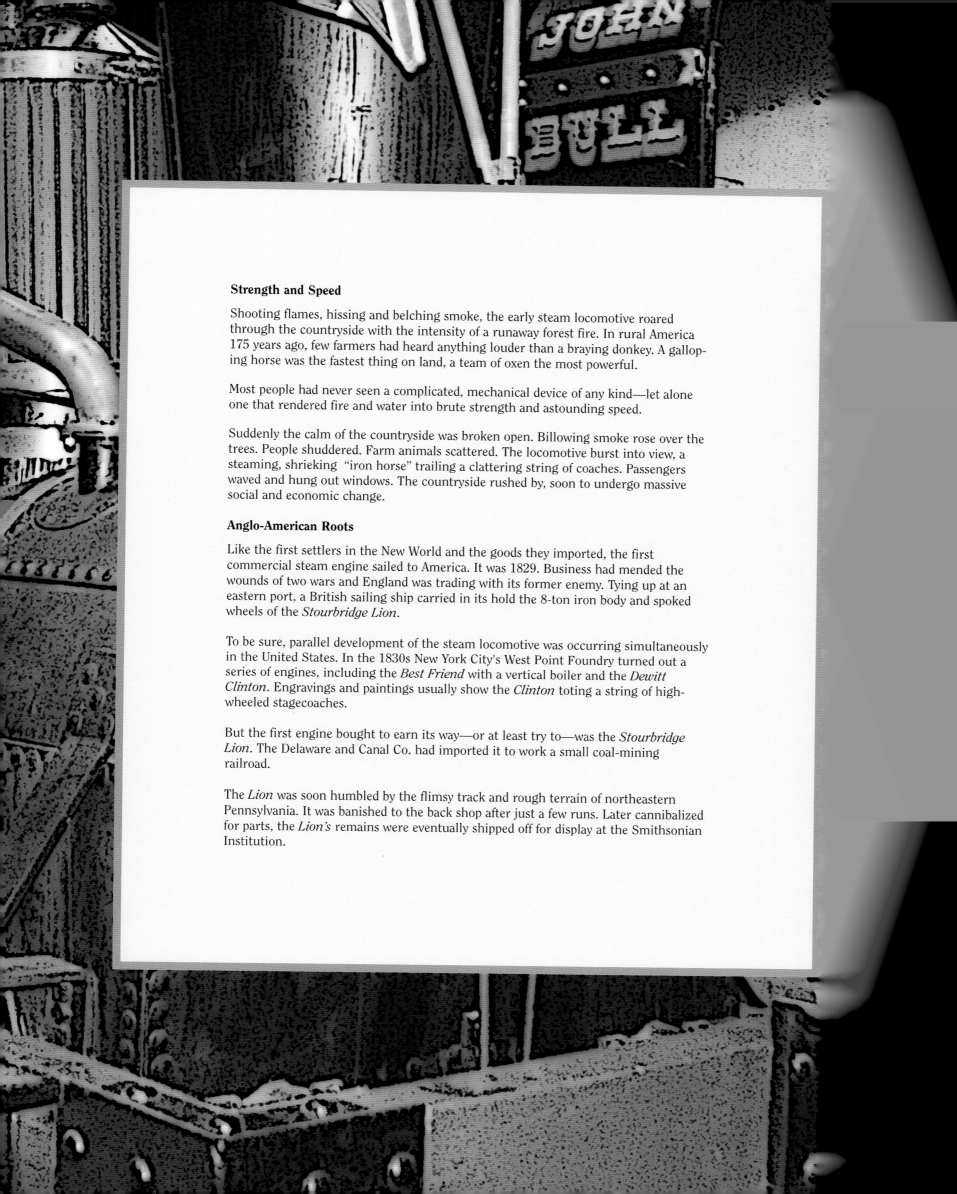

Strength and Speed

Shooting flames, hissing and belching smoke, the early steam locomotive roared through the countryside with the intensity of a runaway forest fire. In rural America 175 years ago, few farmers had heard anything louder than a braying donkey. A galloping horse was the fastest thing on land, a team of oxen the most powerful.

Most people had never seen a complicated, mechanical device of any kind—let alone one that rendered fire and water into brute strength and astounding speed.

Suddenly the calm of the countryside was broken open. Billowing smoke rose over the trees. People shuddered. Farm animals scattered. The locomotive burst into view, a steaming, shrieking "iron horse" trailing a clattering string of coaches. Passengers waved and hung out windows. The countryside rushed by, soon to undergo massive social and economic change.

Anglo-American Roots

Like the first settlers in the New World and the goods they imported, the first commercial steam engine sailed to America. It was 1829. Business had mended the wounds of two wars and England was trading with its former enemy. Tying up at an eastern port, a British sailing ship carried in its hold the 8-ton iron body and spoked wheels of the *Stourbridge Lion*.

To be sure, parallel development of the steam locomotive was occurring simultaneously in the United States. In the 1830s New York City's West Point Foundry turned out a series of engines, including the *Best Friend* with a vertical boiler and the *Dewitt Clinton*. Engravings and paintings usually show the *Clinton* toting a string of high-wheeled stagecoaches.

But the first engine bought to earn its way—or at least try to—was the *Stourbridge Lion*. The Delaware and Canal Co. had imported it to work a small coal-mining railroad.

The *Lion* was soon humbled by the flimsy track and rough terrain of northeastern Pennsylvania. It was banished to the back shop after just a few runs. Later cannibalized for parts, the *Lion's* remains were eventually shipped off for display at the Smithsonian Institution.

Undaunted by initial failure, Americans imported yet another British locomotive in 1831, the 10-ton *John Bull*. Built by Robert Stephenson of Newcastle, often credited as the inventor of the steam locomotive, the *John Bull* had two pairs of wooden driving wheels. But, just as with the *Lion*, the *Bull* was no match for the rough and tumble of frontier America.

Train of Inventions

The Camden & Amboy Railroad of New Jersey, the *John Bull's* owner, quickly recast replacement wheels of iron. More important, to keep *John Bull* from jumping the track and tumbling into the woods, the railroad came up with an ingeniuous and far-reaching innovation: a pair of pilot wheels was added in front of the driving wheels.

These flexible wheels guided the engine into sharp curves, keeping its rigid drivers on the rails. Called a pilot truck, the innovation was distinctly American. It was the first in a long train of steam-driven inventions that would stretch from cowcatchers and air brakes to automatic stokers and steam whistles.

By the mid-19th century, just 20 years after the first commercial steam locomotive, 9,000 miles of track had been laid on the Eastern Seaboard. By the Civil War, every state east of the Mississippi River was linked in a 30,000-mile national network.

More American innovations, like the steel T-rail, reduced derailments, minimized friction and increased speed, making steam trains more efficient. All the while American railroad construction continued at a breathtaking pace, surpassing a quarter million miles of track at the end of World War I. The steam train was so vital to "progress" that cities and towns first begged, then bribed, railroad companies to route new lines their way. If that didn't work, many trackless towns funded and built branches to connect with trunk lines.

From *Tom Thumb* to Mastodons

Keeping pace with explosive rail expansion, the steam engine eventually reached gargantuan proportions. *Tom Thumb*, a diminutive Baltimore & Ohio Railroad steam engine that broke down in 1830 during its famous race with a horse, weighed just 10,000 lbs. Measuring only 13 ft. 2 in., it had four small wheels and a 52-gallon boiler.

From that humble beginning, locomotives grew exponentially. When the *Empire State Express* hit 112.5 mph in Batavia, NY, establishing the 1892 world speed record, it was

pulled by No. 999, a big "American Class" locomotive that weighed 204,000 lbs., stretched nearly 60 ft., and carried 3,000 gallons of water in its boiler.

With each new design, the steam locomotive grew more complex. The railroads themselves or the big locomotive makers—American Locomotive Works (ALCO), Baldwin and Lima—assigned names to the new engines, often as impressive as the machines themselves. Mikado, Mogul and Decapod... Mastodon, Northern, Mountain and more. They were magical sounding monikers. They did little, however, to enlighten anyone unfamiliar with the locomotive.

To address the confusion, the numerical Whyte Classification System was devised in the 1900s. Under this system, each pair of locomotive wheels was assigned a number in sequential order. So, a big Northern locomotive with two pairs of pilot wheels up front (4), four pairs of driving wheels (8) and two pairs of trailing wheels (4) was designated simply as "4-8-4".

The Northern type was first built for the Northern Pacific Railroad, but many railroads had other names for this classic steam engine. The New York Central called it a "Niagara." In the South it was the "Dixie" or the "Potomac." An engine foreman working in a Santa Fe roundhouse might not know a "Niagara" from a "Northern." But say, "4-8-4" and the locomotive type was instantly recognizable.

Speedsters and Heavy Haulers

With giant driving wheels over seven feet high, sleek and often clad in streamlined shells, the last of the great passenger train locomotives were built for extreme speed. The fastest unofficial record of 125 mph for a steam train was set on a "Hiawatha" express on the Milwaukee Road between Chicago and St. Paul.

By contrast, freight engines, the real heavy haulers, were built for traction and strength. Although important, speed was usually secondary to power. To gain traction and increase the ratio of wheel surface to rail, freight engines generally had more but smaller driving wheels.

Reaching its apex in the mid-20th century, the massive, articulated freight locomotives were so gigantic that they required hinges in the middle to negotiate tight curves.

The most famous of these engines, the Big Boy 4-8-8-4 of the Union Pacific Railroad, weighed over one million pounds and measured 132 ft. long. A similar articulated locomotive, the Allegheny of the Chesapeake & Ohio Railroad, had an astonishing 7,498 horsepower. These engines made short work out of pulling a train of 150 freight cars.

The roaring firebox in many giant locomotives was as big as a kitchen. Some of the engines burned oil piped from the tender into the firebox. In others a mechanical, screw-type stoker fed coal automatically into the firebox. The fire was so immense, no human could shovel fast enough to keep it going.

Although steam locomotives required constant maintenance—from New York to Chicago, engines and crews might be changed several times—great strides in efficiency were made in the final years. The Santa Fe Railroad entrusted a single 2-10-2 locomotive to pull its legendary *Chief* trains over the entire 1,700-mile route from Chicago to Los Angles. The engines performed ably which was mandatory. The *Chief* and *Super Chief* were the preferred trains of Hollywood stars and other demanding, well-heeled clientele.

Full Steam Ahead—To Last Gasp!

Despite these advances, the sun was setting on steam. It was to go down fast. Just prior to World War II, the new diesel engines began making inroads on the steam locomotive. The railroads liked what they saw. The attack at Pearl Harbor, however, put a hold on all new locomotive construction.

Once the war ended, the onslaught of diesels quickly routed steam. The changeover was so fast and so complete, that by 1960 the steam locomotive made its last regularly scheduled run on a major U.S. railroad.

Many factors conspired to doom the steam locomotive. Diesels were more efficient and cheaper. They ran great distances without stopping for water or fuel. Routine maintenance was minimal and comparatively easy on diesels. Suddenly the huge, costly infrastructure of coaling stations, water towers, back shops, turntables and roundhouses became superfluous.

The cost of labor, always the most expensive factor in any operation, was drastically reduced. Entire trades and specialized skills vanished overnight. Even Wall Street ganged up on the dying steam engine.

Worn out by the heavy traffic of the war years, the railroads desperately needed new equipment. Banks and investors were eager to underwrite the cost of the modern, and easily repossessed, new diesels. But for railroads that still wanted steam, outmoded technology was a tough sell.

The diesel locomotive enjoyed yet another great advantage. Every steam locomotive coupled to a train required a separate crew. A pair of double-header steam engines on the front required two separate crews. With the diesel, however, one crew could control multiple engines.

Saving Grace

In retrospect, the diesel engine may have rescued the railroads. Without its efficiency and savings, the railroads might have succumbed to the hammerlock of onerous, out-dated regulation and truck and airplane competition on heavily subsidized highways and airports.

With the end of regulation, railroads are enjoying a great resurgence. Even rail fans, who left the railroads when steam engines did, have come back. Their first love may be steam, but many find beauty and excitement in the once lowly diesel.

As this book shows, sometimes they can have both, courtesy of the many railroad museums and dedicated steam preservationists across the land.

Steam trains have always captivated artists. England's J. M. Turner was one of the first to capture the mystical quality of a speeding locomotive. Impressionist Claude Monet celebrated the shimmering violets and blues of smoky steam engines. In a stunning 1854 landscape of rustic America that hangs in Washington's National Gallery, George Inness portrayed the steam locomotive as a beautiful but unstoppable agent of change.

In these paintings commissioned for this book, author/artist Charles Fulkerson demonstrates the continued fascination that painters have for the beauty and power of trains.

Daylight Sensation!

Superlatives are the rule when describing the "Daylight" streamliner that ran between Los Angeles and San Francisco for 34 years. Even to the casual observer, the train was striking. To steam fans, art deco lovers and the Southern Pacific Railroad, the Daylight was "The most beautiful train in the world."

Not only was the train gorgeous, but its route hugging the calendar-like Pacific coastline was, and still is, among the most scenic in the world. Here it is shown charging across a trestle north of Santa Barbara. The train was inaugurated in 1937. Its sleek design and brilliant colors were a good antidote to the dreary Depression years.

The big 4-8-4 Northern locomotives that pulled the train were built by Lima and clad in brilliant orange steel skirts. The boiler was black and red, with a silver nose and an orange and silver cowcatcher. This vivid color scheme was extended to the tender and 12 cars with panoramic windows

A Train That Rolls On!

The train was an immediate sensation. It could have been marketed by any name that bespoke elegance and speed. Instead it was simply "the Daylight," because it made the 470 mile trip between Los Angeles and San Francisco during the day. The Daylight spawned similar trains on other Southern Pacific lines. Because the Southern Pacific Northern fireboxes burned oil, not coal, the trains stayed clean.

Today, the Daylight route is still traversed by Amtrak, but the brilliant color scheme and mighty Northerns were long retired when Amtrak took over in the early 1970s. No. 4449, one of the original orange and silver Northerns, was revived in 1976 to celebrate the American Bicentennial. Later, in a stroke of civic foresight, the city of Portland, Oregon, bought the engine and cars. The Daylight colors were restored, and the entire train still makes excursion runs

Meet the Real "Polar Express"

Pounding the frozen farmland and rattling the windowpanes, big No. 1225 rockets a "North Pole Express" train across the Michigan prairie on a frigid December afternoon.

It's 2005. The muscular, 2-8-4 steam locomotive is 64 years old, but pulling its sold-out, 10-car train is a romp in the park. This venerable engine from the old Pierre Marquette Railroad is bound for a trackside Santa Claus stationed at the Saginaw County Fairgrounds.

No. 1225 is so impressive that its reputation has reached Hollywood. When the computer animation for Tom Hanks' "Polar Express" film was made in 2004, the studio honored No. 1225 as the real-life prototype for the animated version. Fittingly, and by chance alone, the locomotive's number coincides with Christmas Day.

Arriving at the Steam Railroading Institute (SRI) in Owosso, Michigan, moviemakers poured over the engine's blueprints, then photographed and recorded No. 1225 in action. In the film, which has grossed $300 million worldwide for Hollywood, moviegoers hear the chuff and hiss, roar and whistle of the real engine.

Despite the fame and glory the engine has earned, it hasn't always been full steam ahead for No. 1225. Built by Lima Locomotive Works in 1941, the engine was retired only 10 years later. Still in its youth, No. 1225 was headed for oblivion. Michigan State University intervened, convincing the railroad to donate the steam engine for display.

Later, engineering students dreamed of overhauling the locomotive for full operation. Overwhelmed by the massive restoration needed to bring the 600-ton locomotive back to life, they unwittingly created an eyesore instead. Eventually, No. 1225 was moved to the SRI. "The engine was in acute disarray," recalled one of the hundreds of volunteers at SRI. "It looked like it had leprosy."

After nearly 40 years and thousands of volunteer hours later, the engine retook the rails. Was it all worth it? Just ask the thousands of gleeful children inspired by the might and majesty of No. 1225 during 18 consecutive, sold-out Santa trips from Thanksgiving to Christmas. Steam's finest hour is still playing every year in southern Michigan!

Steam Still Rules the Rails

Rounding a graceful, half-mile arc, No. 734 of the Western Maryland Scenic Railroad lugs a long passenger train of modern day rail fans through the Allegheny Mountains.

This setting, Helmstetter's Curve near Cumberland, Maryland, has been a favorite of professional and amateur rail photographers for half a century. Here, the jade green fields and late fall colors of the Cash Valley contrast with the sun dappled burgundy coaches and 2-8-0 Consolidation working the curve.

One of Maryland's most acclaimed tourist attractions, the Western Maryland Scenic Railroad runs regularly scheduled excursions between Cumberland and Frostburg. Every year it attracts thousands from around the world who crave the thrill of live steam trains.

So popular is this steam train that even locals routinely show up twice a day for its passing through the mountains. They, and those aboard, drink in the nostalgic sight and sound of the Baldwin locomotive, while savoring the pungent fragrance of burning coal, hot oil and steam.

In its heyday, the old Western Maryland Railroad was renowned for Fire Ball Fast Freight service between Baltimore and points west. No. 734 wears the Fire Ball symbol on its tender, a tribute to the seemingly endless parade of big steam freights that once lumbered around this curve.

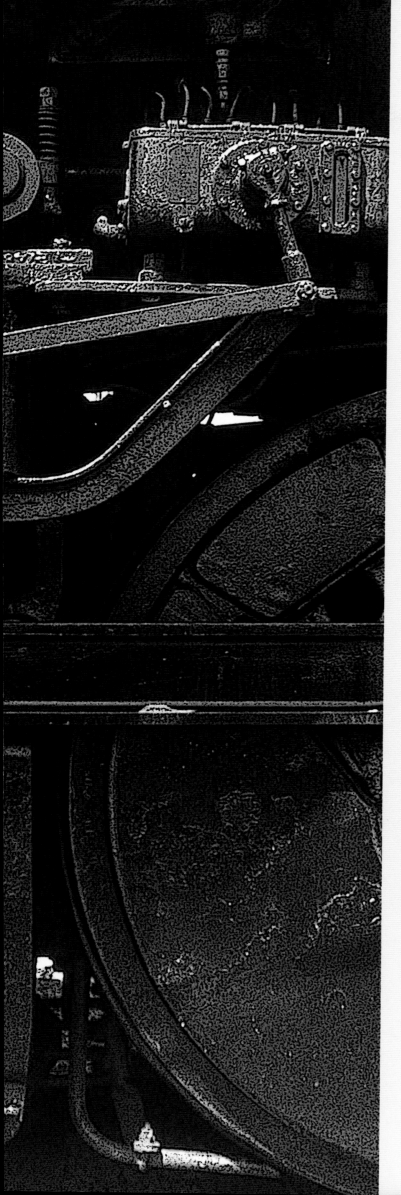

Chapter One:
Glory vs. Sacrifice...

The glorious names in American steam railroading are a "Who's Who" of U.S. politics, finance, industry, and even art. Influential lawyers Abraham Lincoln and Steven A. Douglas defended and advanced railroad expansion. At opposite ends of the country, California Governor Leland Stanford and financier J.P. Morgan bankrolled construction. Rail barons like Cornelius Vanderbilt and Jay Gould consolidated railroads with the first mega-mergers. Retooling the emerging steel industry, Andrew Carnegie rose from the Pittsburgh slums to amass a fortune. He forged a million miles of steel rail. In turn, the endless trains of iron ore, coke and coal that fed the Carnegie mills polished the rails. Later, celebrated industrial designers Henry Dreyfuss and Raymond Lowey brought dazzling art deco designs to railroading in the 20th century, turning the steam engine into a fashion statement.

It's a cliché to say the accomplishments and exploits of these individuals were possible because of the sacrifice and daring of everyday railroaders. Nevertheless it's true. Hundreds, perhaps thousands, of Chinese immigrants died blasting the first transcontinental railroad through the High Sierra Mountains. In exchange for a few silver dollars and a bottle of whiskey many workman gave up their lives spanning great rivers and tunneling through the Rockies. And once the railroads were built, keeping the trains running was equally harrowing.

Magnificent Machines and Men...

Pride and Dedication

In the 19th century and well into the early 1900s, thousands of trainmen perished in railroad accidents, wrecks and disasters of epic proportions. Train travel today is the safest mode of transportation, but early on, railroads were seemingly cavalier about the carnage on the rails. In 1888 alone, 2,070 railroaders were killed on the job, and another 20,148 were maimed and injured. Toward the end of the 19th century, the invention of modern knuckle couplers and Westinghouse air brakes greatly reduced the human toll of railroading. Long hours, unpredictable scheduling and the hazards of a dangerous job continued to play havoc with the lives of railroad workers. Through it all, railroaders then, and now, have maintained a high degree of pride and dedication, uncommon in most other industries.

© Charles Fulkerson Jr.

Left:
Simmering in the late autumn sun, a steam engine on the Western Maryland Scenic Railroad in Cumberland has just completed a run up the Allegheny Mountains. The 3,500 h.p. locomotive burns 4 tons of coal on every 30-mile run.

Opposite:
From his perch in the right side of the cab, an engineer awaits the "Highball."

Overleaf pages 24-25:
A trainman climbs down from a locomotive after installing a white flag on the boiler lantern. White flags indicate a special run. This ALCO steam engine operates on the Connecticut Valley Railroad in Essex, Connecticut.

Overleaf pages 26-27:
The nearly empty coalbunker on No. 97 gets a concerned glance from the engineer. The locomotive is heading for home in Essex, Connecticut.

Labor of Love

Steam locomotive maintenance has always been labor intensive. The old photographs of proud engineers with oilcans in hand were not just for show. Thousands of working parts must be lubricated constantly, many by hand, others by oil injected into the steam. Even when steam engines were new, overhauls were routine. For volunteers at the working steam museums and tourist lines, caring for the aged locomotives is a labor of love. After the Steam Age passed, all steam locomotive works closed. So, original parts are scarce or nonexistent. Consequently, replacement parts and even tools must be custom-made. The rebuilding of a Baldwin Consolidation by the Western Maryland Scenic Railroad is typical of the massive work needed to revive a decrepit steam locomotive. Over 90 percent of the replacement parts for the 1916 engine had to be machined in the shops of the tourist hauling line.

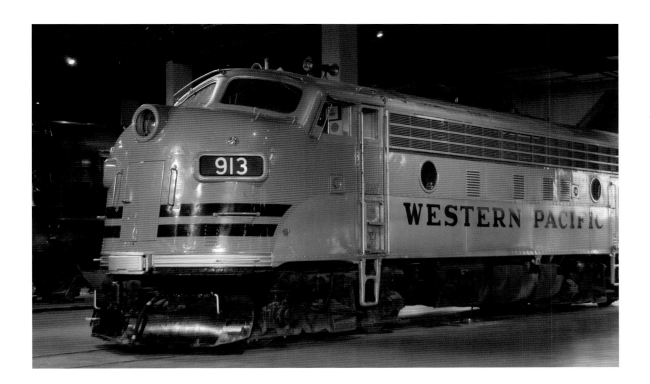

During the great steam engine die-off of the 1950s, nostalgic rail fans organized "last run" excursions for the doomed locomotives. The outpouring of public inter-est engendered many of the superb railroad museums and operating steam tourist lines that flourish today across the United States and Canada. In a tribute to their heritage, a few major railroads also operated occasional steam engine excursions. Led by two train-loving executives who were also brothers, Graham and Robert Claytor, the Southern and Norfolk & Western Railroads were dedicated steam preservationists. Eventually, the brothers retired, the two railroads merged into the Norfolk Southern system, and the steam engines went cold. Of the major U.S. railroads only the Union Pacific still operates a steam excursion program today. Led by its magnificent 4-6-6-4 Challenger—one of the largest of all steam locomotives—the railroad wins customers, friends and publicity with regular excursions across its great system.

Chapter Two:
Live Steam...

The steam engine was, and is, a highly volatile machine. Coal and water that fuel the locomotive are relatively stable—until the two are superheated. At that point, if the water level over the roaring firebox drops too low, the boiler crown sheet melts. Superheated water then pours into the scorching firebox, exploding and turning the locomotive into a bombshell. Constant vigilance in the cab is demanded of both the engineer and fireman. Although common in the Steam Age, this cataclysmic reaction has occurred only once during the modern era of live steam preservation, thanks to the watchful eyes in the cab by both engineer and fireman. Nevertheless, because of the inherent risk of operating steam trains, insurance on most tourist lines and excursions runs is astronomical. Most lines would have folded long ago, if not for a legion of volunteers and generous contributors

Steam Revival...

Boyhood Dream Goes Up in Steam!

Like a boy closing the attic door on his toy trains when it's suppertime, employees at the East Broad Top Railroad & Coal Co. (EBT) knocked off work for dinner one evening in April 1956. They expected only a furlough, due to slack demand for coal. Everything was left in order. Machine shop and tools, roundhouse and roundtable, switchyard and steam locomotives—all were cleaned, oiled, greased and ready to run. But no one came back. The coal-dependent EBT shut down for good. It was sold for scrap value, remaining in a state of suspended animation until 1960.

In a remarkable turn of events, the scrap dealer turned out to be a rail fan. Legend has it that Nick Kovalchick, son of immigrants, never had model trains because his parents were too poor to afford them. The EBT fulfilled his boyhood dreams. The railroad reopened and has operated for the past half century. It may be the finest example of a complete, working steam railroad in America today. It is a National Historic Landmark. General manager Stanley Hall noted that the wealthy Kovalchick named No. 12, one of EBT's steam engines, "Millie," after his then young daughter. "About that time he'd made his first million," chuckled Hall, recalling the EBT's savior and benefactor. Today, the non-profit railroad rolls on, still owned by the farsighted Kovalchick family and supported by ticket fares and the generosity of thousands of donors and volunteers.

Overleaf pages 42-43:

No. 14 pulls in next to EBT's concrete coal dock. A waterspout for filling the tender is just to the left of the engine headlight.

Overleaf pages 44-45:

Like a railroad rush hour, two of the EBT's Baldwin-built Mikado locomotives line up at the station awaiting the Highball.

Right:

Filled with activity, the EBT yard readies one train for departure, while the combine car from another train has just pulled in.

From Black Diamonds to Steam Lovers

Operations on the EBT Railroad have changed some from the railroad's 80-year history as a narrow gauge coal feeder for the Pennsylvania Railroad. Back then, the 33-mile, 3-foot-gauge railroad hauled primarily coal, with some freight, mail, and passengers. Because the railroad is now a tourist line, operations focus on passenger trains. Every summer season, the railroad steams up, transporting thousands of tourists, steam lovers and rail fans. Its 10-mile roundtrip route runs through the scenic Aughwick Valley near Rockhill Furnace in south central Pennsylvania. The railroad even has its own support group, the Friends of East Broad Top Museum at Robertsdale, Pennsylvania.

Above:
On the ready track, a locomotive prepares to depart. The narrow gauge engine is about two-thirds the size of comparable standard gauge locomotives, making the fireman appear much larger than he is. EBT's distance between rails is 36 inches. Standard gauge is 56.5 inches.

Old and Older

The arches of the East Broad Top brick roundhouse frame an old 1950s diesel
electric switch engine. Chartered in 1856 as a coal hauler, the EBT built this
exquisite eight-stall, brick roundhouse around 1900. It's still in use today, housing
the railroad's six Baldwin-built steam engines. The roundhouse is served by the
recently restored and fully operational Armstrong turntable. At the end of its run,
a locomotive proceeds to one of the yard tracks facing the Armstrong turntable.
The turntable platform is swung into position to align with the track, and the
locomotive runs on to it. The locomotive is then swung to one of the tracks
leading into the roundhouse. On most steam railroads, roundhouse personnel
serviced the engine, cleaned the firebox, and oiled and greased the running gear.
Major overhauls were sometimes done in the roundhouse or in adjoining buildings with cranes and pits between the rails for reaching the undercarriage of the
locomotive.

Above:
This M-6 Plymouth-
built 14-ton diesel
engine saw service in
a stone quarry before-
coming to the East
Broad Top Railroad.

Left:
Headed for the round-house, an EBT switch engine will roll onto the wood and rail deck of the turntable platform. The stone building at the right is a 200-year-old farm-house that preceded the railroad.

Below:
A pile of stone separates a time-worn group of out buildings at East Broad Top. The stone will be spread as ballast between the tracks.

Above:
This pressure gauge was a source of constant concern when boilers supplied steam to the shop's stationary steam engine. In the Steam Age, stationary engines, which were fixed in place, were found in many factories and mills.

Below:
An elaborate system of overhead belts and pulleys transferred power from the stationary engine to the heavy machinery on the shop floor.

"Do It Better and Faster Right Here"

Looking almost like they were left a half-century ago, the machine shops of the East Broad Top Railroad are still intact. Dozens of men once worked the machine shops, repairing and rebuilding the railroad's engines and rolling stock. According to EBT general manager Stanley Hall, they were part of a 500-man workforce employed on the coal-hauling short-line in its prime. They included engine and train crew, yardmen, coal miners, office help and shop workers. The extensive shops were powered by a two-cylinder, coal-fired stationary steam engine. Like many old shops of that era powered by water wheels or steam engines, an elaborate system of overhead belts and pulleys brought power to individual machines.

When one of the railroad's locomotives broke down, fixing it was not a simple matter of ordering new parts and waiting until they arrived. "The steam locomotive is pretty much a custom-built piece of machinery," explained Tom Diehl, a machine shop guide and volunteer from the Friends of East Broad Top. "Most likely Baldwin didn't have the parts you wanted in stock. Plus in those days, there was much more of a self-sufficient attitude that, we can do it better or faster right here." To that end, EBT shops had a full complement of belt-driven machines needed to fabricate or repair nearly every part of a steam engine.

Above:
This lathe-like machine is a Wheel Turner to grind true both steel car wheels and the locomotive wheels and tires. Locomotive drivers were fitted with a thinner and softer metal tire to provide more traction.

Running through the Twilight of Steam!

In the twilight of steam, the East Broad Top Railroad stuck with its all steam roster. Six Baldwin-built Mikado engines did the heavy hauling. Baldwin applied the Mikado appellation generically to all its 2-8-2 locomotives, after selling some of the first to Japan Railways at the turn of the 19th century. (Both the well-known Gilbert & Sullivan opera and the locomotive take their name from Mikado, the ancient Japanese term for emperor.) The EBT's Mikados were good runners. They were built new for the railroad between 1911-1920. The two middle driving wheels on both sides of these locomotive are so-called "blind drivers," without flanges against the inner side of the rail. These flangeless drivers make the engine less rigid and better able to negotiate sharp curves.

No matter how well they run, however, all steam engines are labor intensive to maintain. One senior volunteer at Michigan's Steam Railroading Institute estimated that for every one hour of running time, 10 hours of back shop work are required to keep the engine in top shape. That estimate applies to a massive 2-8-4 Berkshire steam locomotive, and not a narrow gauge Mikado. Nevertheless, the size of the EBT shop complex is a true indication of how much work was needed to maintain the small railroad's modest roster of locomotives and rolling stock.

Opposite page:
Much of the work at the EBT shops was done by hand, as indicated by this heavy, forged-steel vise bolted to a workbench.

Above:
Dozens of steam engine hand wrenches and car tools hang where they were left when the last workers went home for dinner years ago.

Right:
Old axles and wheels sit on the shop floor waiting for repairs. A machinist getting a foot squashed under a set of wheels like these would feel as if an elephant stepped on him.

Chapter Three:
Travel and Travail...

After surviving the stormy North Atlantic Ocean in steerage, European immigrants bound for America's wide-open spaces were promised the comfort and security of train travel. Railroads recruited settlers with newspaper ads both here and abroad. They extolled inexpensive land and cheap easy passage to the homestead of their dreams. The reality was harsher. Shipping people long distance then was a big and profitable business, just as with any other commodity. Like today, pairs of seats flanked an open aisle stretching the length of the car. But passengers were jammed in; there was no privacy for women and families. One 19th century wag referred to the aisles as extended spittoons.

Passenger coaches were loud, bumpy, and drafty. In the heat of summer, engine smoke and soot billowed in through the windows. Tobacco smoke, body odor, and whiskey fumes wafted out. Lamp oil, from whales or coal, provided greasy light. In summer, passengers baked. In winter, they shivered. With windows shut to keep out cold and snow, smoky braziers filled with coal embers heated the pungent inside air. Perhaps comfortable compared to a rocking stagecoach or pitching ship, early train travel was a trial for most.

On the Move

Before baggage cars, passengers hauled their belongings, and in some cases all their worldly goods, up the steep stairs into the coaches. Navigating the aisles was a challenge. Whatever didn't fit on overhead racks was jammed into the center passageway or car vestibules. As often as not, caged chickens and tethered livestock rode right along with the passengers. Realizing they could charge more if passengers and their live freight or heavy trunks were separated, baggage cars were added to trains, relieving the congestion. Initially, train travel was lauded as an extension of democratic ideals. Passengers were free to sit where they wanted. Rich or poor rode together. That was to soon change. Car builders and railroads discovered a gold mine when they segregated passengers into First and Second Class and charged accordingly. On the low end of service, racially segregated "Jim Crow" cars were the norm in much of the country.

Right:
Hand-drawn baggage cart and horse-drawn freight wagon are displayed at the Sacramento freight depot.

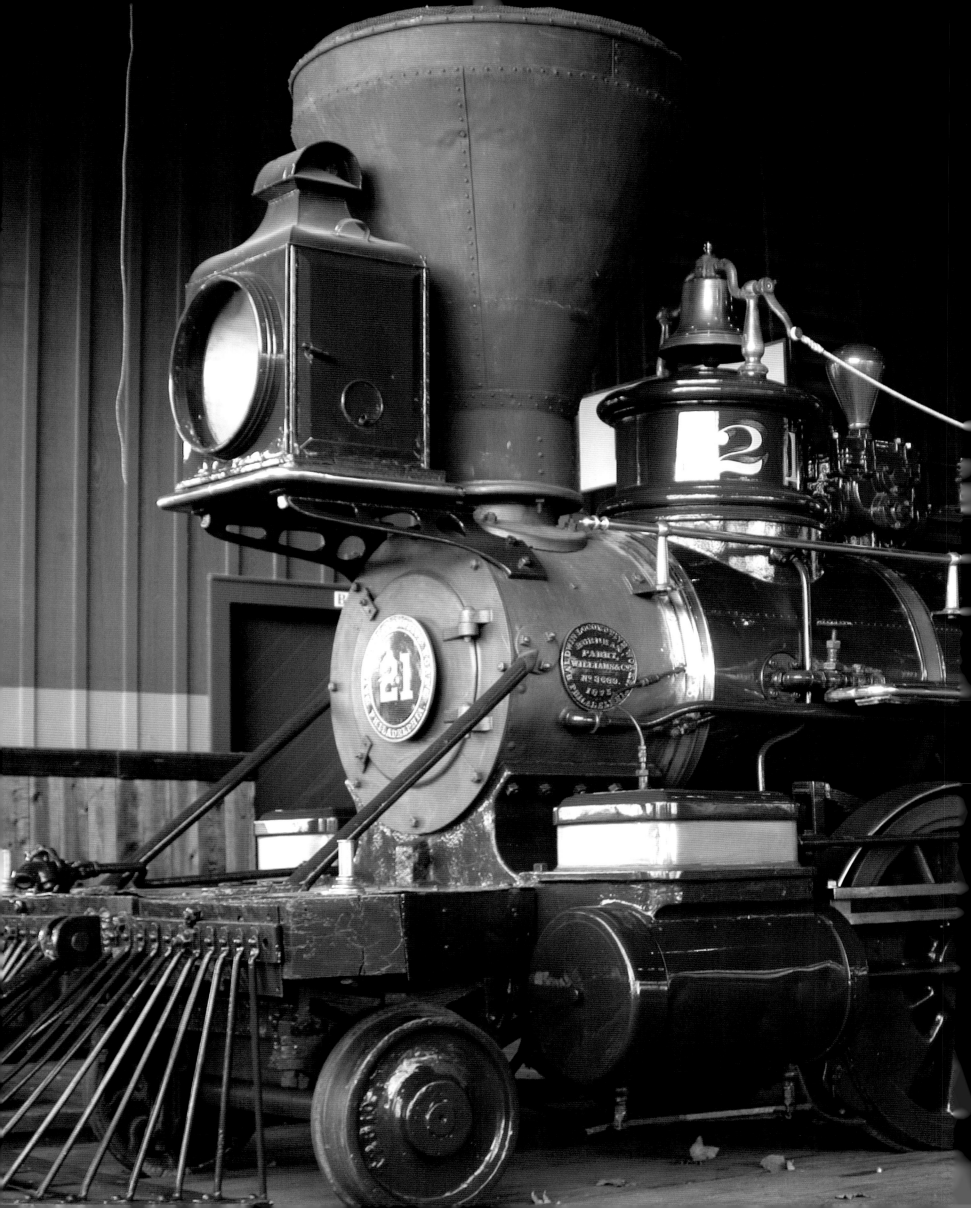

Left:
Less than 30 steam locomotives built before 1880 still survive. The Virginia & Truckee No. 21 is one of them. Built in 1875, the 2-4-0 locomotive last operated in San Francisco in 1953. Like many of the early locomotives, this engine burned wood, not coal.

Left:
A manual typewriter and train order tablet sit at the station agent's desk..

Below:
A typical office in the reconstructed Central Pacific Station.

Tough Duty in Spartan Quarters

Station agents and their staff, if any, worked out of relatively spartan offices. Railroads spared no expense on opulent, big city stations; but they made up for it out on the line. In flyspeck towns, the agent was the only man on duty. In remote mountain and prairie locations, the agent's family often took up residence above the station. Even when most trains roared by without slowing, the agent was kept hopping. He was a vital link in the vast network of unending telegraph lines that stretched along the tracks. When not tending to tickets or freight, the agent received and transcribed train orders. After receiving a telegraphed order, the agent typed out the message on the fly.

Eat and Run

Before George Pullman turned his genius to onboard dining, passenger trains stopped at stations for meals. Famished passengers bolted from the trains as they pulled in, dashing toward the food. Restaurants like the Central Pacific's Silver Palace were engulfed by the stampede. Men ran to the bar for food and drink. Women and children rushed for the tables. Typically, trains did not stop long before continuing on. Unless the station was a division point where steam engines were changed, or a large station where passengers changed trains, there was no time for leisurely dining. Later on, another entrepreneur, Fred Harvey, revolutionized station dining on the Santa Fe Railroad. Harvey upgraded food and service dramatically. He hired unmarried, attractive young women from the East to waitress. "Harvey Girls" became the hallmark of his Harvey House restaurants and the wives of many patrons.

Waiting

Unlike passenger cars where the sexes were not separated, some railroad stations provided separate waiting rooms for men and women. In the Sacramento Station, the general waiting room was relatively spacious with polished wooden benches. Since chewing and smoking tobacco were favored by men, spittoons were probably common. Sawdust may have been spread on the floor to sop up spittle that missed. A nearby Lady's Waiting Room offered both privacy and heat. A simple dresser with mirror, towels, basin and porcelain water pitcher gave women a chance to freshen up before boarding the train.

"Railroad Time" Was On Time

In stations, clocks were everywhere—on walls and desks, in bell towers and pocket vests. This imposing wall case clock from the Atchison, Topeka & Santa Fe Railroad underscores the importance of time keeping. For precise time, three pendulums governed hour and minute hand, second hand, and strike. The clock called attention to its vital function with a handsome hardwood case, glass front, finials, and a sculpted ornamental frieze. On transcontinental railroads like the Santa Fe, accurate time keeping was especially important. The railroad traversed three time zones. Named for the Santa Fe Trail, which it followed to the Southwest—and not the capital of New Mexico—the Santa Fe was one of the most colorful and profitable of all transcontinentals. It stretched from Chicago to Texas, to the Grand Canyon, and on to California, with terminals at Los Angeles, San Diego, and San Francisco Bay. A rival of the Southern Pacific Railroad, the Santa Fe is now a "Fallen Flag" railroad. It merged with the Burlington Northern to form the BNSF Railroad, the nation's second largest. Southern Pacific, another Fallen Flag, was eventually folded into the Union Pacific Railroad, America's biggest.

Romans, Ruts and Rails

The standard gauge, or space, between the two rails of a track is four feet, eight and one-half inches. This worldwide standard is nearly universal.

The origin of standard gauge is much discussed, but legend holds that it evolved from the Romans. The space between Roman chariot wheels was supposedly four feet, eight and one-half inches.

When the first tracks were laid two millennia later, ruts from those chariot wheels were still visible in the ancient Roman roads of England. When setting the gauge, the English merely followed the ruts in the road.

From the first crude tracks fashioned from iron strips on flimsy wooden rails and logs, tracks gradually morphed into ever-heavier iron, then steel T-shaped rails. Hefty spikes anchored rails to large creosoted slabs of lumber usually called ties or sleepers. In Europe and increasingly in the United States, concrete ties have replaced the wooden ones.

There are two significant exceptions to standard gauge, most notably, narrow gauge. Smaller gauge railroads were cheaper to construct and were once widespread on mountain lines, logging routes, mines and sugar cane fields of Hawaii and the Caribbean.

Broad gauge, the other major exception, is slightly larger than standard. Today, Spain and Russia are two countries still using this gauge. After the invasion of Napoleon, the Russians laid broad gauge to forestall future invaders from running military trains unimpeded across the border.

Above:
The narrow gauge "Silver State" is a first class passenger car built by the Nevada Central Railroad.

Narrow Gauge Niche

Narrow gauge railroads were common in the American West in the late 19th and early 20th centuries. Many of them were captive to specific industries like mining, logging or ranching. Unlike standard gauge, these lines were not always interconnected. Instead, they hauled their products and passengers to a connection with standard gauge lines where cargo and passengers were reloaded on larger cars. The "Silver State" narrow gauge passenger car at left was constructed in 1881 by the Nevada Central Railroad, which made reload connections with the standard gauge Central Pacific at Austin, Nevada. The car's raised, center roof featured small deck windows that brought in light and ventilation. Another Nevada silver line, the Virginia & Truckee, was standard gauge, interchanging cars with the Central Pacific. The combined passenger and baggage car, or "Combine" at right, was a forerunner of the caboose.

Below:
This combination passenger and baggage Combine was built in 1874.

Overleaf:
The interior of No. 14 featured a painted ceiling cloth, shutters and reversible velvet seats.

Above:
The ornamental interior bulkhead of the Virginia & Truckee No. 16 Combine invites passengers into the attractive seating area.

Backhead Blues...

Taking a Break

Drifting downhill with a short passenger train in tow, No. 40's safety valves are popping with steam, indicating high pressure in the boiler. Located at the top of the steam dome, safety valves automatically release excessive pressure that could blow up the boiler if left unchecked. With a hot fire and a full head of steam, the fireman has earned a break. The running board doors are thrown open, cooling off the cab with a fresh breeze. The backhead, or end of the boiler, is the front wall of the cab. Both backhead and sizzling firebox doors are exposed to the cab interior, raising summertime temperature and humidity to almost unbearable levels. In winter, the backhead and firebox keep the front of the cab toasty, but the rear of the cab is open to the elements. No. 40, a 2-8-0 Consolidation, originally saw service in the South before moving to Pennsylvania's New Hope & Ivyland Railroad.

Left:
Steaming hard, the New Hope & Ivyland No. 40 heads into sun. This venerable locomotive demonstrates the speed and power of an early 20th century locomotive, while pulling a line of filled passenger cars.

Pullman Upgrade

For 90 years the name Pullman was the touchstone for high class railroad passenger service. George Pullman was both entrepreneur and promotional genius. A Canadian designed the first luxury rail car in 1860 for visiting English royalty. When Pullman saw it, he quickly realized that the rich would pay extra to travel in comfort. He founded the Pullman Palace Car Company. True to its name, the early Pullman cars were rolling palaces. Outfitted with rich, mahogany paneling, leaded stained glass, chandeliers, plush carpets, and private bedrooms, the cars were elegant and expensive. They were a refuge for the monied class.

Pullman cars won national acclaim immediately after the Civil War. Abraham Lincoln's influence on early American railroading was pervasive, even in death. George Pullman realized that the slain President's remains could be a boon for business. Pullman arranged for his elegant car to carry the President's body from Washington, D.C., to its grave in Springfield, Illinois. The funeral train made a long, circuitous trip. Thousands viewed the sumptuous Pullman car. George Pullman had engineered a promotional bonanza.

Above:
The elaborate interior and plush seats of a First Class car promise a comfortable ride.

Above:
The observation platform at the end of this narrow gauge car was a favorite place to watch western farms and ranches slip by.

Overleaf:
A passenger train on the narrow gauge East Broad Top Railroad rolls through the mist on an early morning run.

Rolling Pony Express...

Mail Call

Before planes and trucks, railroads carried all the U.S. mail. Over 30,000 U.S. mail workers sorted mail on the move on 700 routes across the country. Most mainline trains had a Railway Post Office (RPO) car located up front behind the engine or baggage cars. Leaving a large city with canvas mailbags stacked to the ceiling, RPO cars functioned as mobile post offices. Working feverishly against the clock and the upcoming stations, RPO clerks were nimble, fast and accurate. They were permitted only 5 mistakes per every 7,000 pieces of sorted mail. Beyond the mountain of mail to sort at the start of the run, mailbags were picked up and dropped off on the fly. As a train approached a station at speed, a clerk extended a hook from the RPO car. When the train whizzed by, the hook snatched the mailbag. Dumped into large trays, the contents of the mailbag were then sorted and stuffed into slots and mailbags for towns and cities along the line. Loaded bags were pitched out when the train passed the appropriate station.

Above:

Looking down on a Great Northern Railroad RPO, the mailbag stand is to the right of the car. In the car's open door, a white hook will extend to grab a mailbag as the car rushes by.

Right and opposite:

RPO clerks filled mail slots for locations along the railroad. Clerks on the Great Northern RPO were fast and accurate.

Photographed at the California State Railroad Museum, Sacramento, CA

Overleaf pages 78-79:
Rolling Restaurants. Galley cooks in a
Santa Fe diner put the finishing touches on the
often elaborate meals served aboard railroad
dining cars.

Dinner on the Diner

The premier experience on any long distance train was a trip to the diner. No stationary restaurant, and certainly no airplane, could ever compare. Picture yourself dining on a crack train of yesteryear. Your place is set with china, heavy silver-plate, crystal and linen. A low-cut spray of fresh flowers is by the window, but does not obscure the view at your elbow. An immaculately dressed and starched waiter serves you a martini or uncorks champagne. You toast the panoramic view of rugged mountains, fertile farms or swirling rapids as your train crosses a swift river below.

The epicurean delights, scratch-made and served with pomp aboard fine diners, surpassed first-class dining on some transatlantic steam ships. Railroads took great pride in regional specialties: French and Praline Toast, Lobster Bisque and Turtle Soup, Duck Cumberland and Rabbit Pie, Filet of Barracuda and Trout Blue, Spinach Florentine and Beef Jardinière, Peach Melba or Marcela Sundae. For the railroads, great diners earned a reputation that attracted passengers. Diners were loss-leaders, but vital to business.

Above:
Fresh flowers adorn the entrance to this diner car— also shown in another view on the previous two pages—at the California State Railroad Museum. On some diners, waiters tapped out first call for dinner on hand held chimes.

Photographed at the Railroad Museum of Pennsylvania, Strasburg, PA

Above:

This simple table for four is probably set for breakfast. French toast, grits, oatmeal, and eggs cooked to order are on the menu. Even today, breakfast, lunch, or dinner on Amtrak's "Empire Builder" and Pacific coast trains is still a treat.

Right:

Preparing for last call, a waiter sets out wine glasses and a bouquet in a silver-plated chalice. Elegant four-star travel in North America is still found aboard the Grandluxe Rail Journeys of the American Orient Express headquartered in Downers Grove, Illinois. This historic car is one of the Sacramento museum's highly prized exhibits.

Sleeping with Mr. Pullman

George Pullman, the legendary sleeping car impresario, leased his sleepers to the railroads. Railroads called for extra cars as needed. The cars were staffed by Pullman. Service was impeccable, accommodations comfortable and sometimes luxurious. Responsibility for the passengers fell to the beloved porter. In the steam era, these men were always black, dignified, and unfailingly courteous and industrious. They had to be. Pullman standards were exacting, and passengers were demanding. A Pullman sleeper was stocked with 360 folded sheets and 200 towels. In a full car, most were in laundry bags by the end of a run. Porters made up all berths and bedrooms, alternately converting daytime chairs to beds and back again daily. Working 400 hours a month for a paltry wage, porters traveled up to 120,000 miles a year. Thousands worked the Pullmans. But, until the Brotherhood of Sleeping Car Porters negotiated better wages and nametags in 1938, all were generically addressed as "George."

Above:
At night, these comfortable chairs aboard a Canadian National Pullman folded down into a lower berth bed. Another bed folded out from the ceiling. Heavy plush curtains were pulled for privacy.

Above:

Beyond making these chairs into beds, porters performed a variety of exacting tasks to keep passengers happy, from warming baby bottles to chilling beer. Two pages in the service manual outlined the Pullman way to serve beer.

Left:

With private sleeping compartments on the right, passengers walking through the train to the diner or bar car passed down this narrow hall.

Above:
The sparkling sinks aboard a Pullman are a tribute to the high standards and pride of sleeping car porters.

Opposite:
Lulled by the clickety-clack of the rails and the silky smooth ride on well-maintained tracks, passengers get a sound night's sleep.

What's in a Name?

Pullman sleepers were as much a part of the aura of train travel as the dining car. The Broadway Limited's deluxe sleepers featured two-level duplex rooms. Some western lines had glass-domed sleepers for passengers to gaze at the stars before retiring. Early sleepers featured a small galley and cook on board. Not satisfied with merely numbering its cars, Pullman named all its sleepers and diners. With thousands of cars, naming was serious business. So serious that Pullman had a Vice President of Nomenclature! Some names were inspired by the Classics — *Archimedes* and *Hyperion*, for instance — and some for places, like *Revelstoke Park* and *Paradise Valley*. Others were named for famous people on the route, such as *James Witcomb Riley* and *Davy Crockett*.

Continuing the tradition, railroads named their best trains. Names conjured up speed and luxury, such as *The 20th Century Limited*. Boarding passengers on the *Century* literally got red carpet treatment. (Every evening before leaving for Chicago, a red carpet was rolled out at Grand Central Station.) Other names were exotic, like the *Orange Blossom Special* or *Wolverine*. Informal monikers applied by passengers poked fun at trains. An Illinois Central Railroad train from "dry" Kentucky into "wet" Illinois was dubbed *The Whiskey Dick*. Meanwhile, the "hound dog" in the Elvis Presley hit song actually refers to a gulf train derisively known as the *Hound Dog*.

Chapter Four:
The Evolution
of Steam...

Steam locomotives today are cherished. Engines still running are living relics, cared for like the survivors of a nearly extinct species, which of course they are. Viewed through a haze of nostalgia in museums like the Smithsonian or operating on tourist lines, it's easy to forget that in their day they were quite literally, engines of commerce—the work horses of the economy.

If their robber-baron owners cherished them, it was solely for profit. Fast, new locomotives were glamorous. But soon enough they joined the ranks of thousands of other steam engines. All labored relatively unnoticed simply because they were so commonplace. Steam engines were a necessity. They were also loud, dirty and smoky. In their prime, they were mainly loved by their engineers and generations of boys yearning to take the throttle.

Deluxe trains and the opening of new railroads did stir the public. The 20th Century and Broadway Limiteds, competing trains on rival railroads, were often celebrated in the press. The Golden Spike, joining the transcontinental railroad in 1867, was cause for national jubilation. This chapter traces steam evolution from construction of the transcontinental railroad to dieseldom and the beginning of the end of steam.

Building the Transcontinental Railroad...

Bringing America Together!

As a monumental, national undertaking, few projects rival construction of the first transcontinental railroad. Driven more by politics than profit, construction was started by President Abraham Lincoln in 1862. The railroad would tether the burgeoning, gold-rich California to the Union.

Although not finished until four years after the Civil War, its construction helped bind a war-ravaged people. Captained by retired Union Army officers, Confederate and Federal veterans worked side by side, along with Irish immigrants.
Once completed in 1869, the line put an end to harrowing, "prairie schooner" wagon trains across the Great Plains and high mountains to California. Equally hazardous ocean passage around the tip of South America was also curtailed.

Going to Pieces!

California had already built a significant railroad network before the Civil War. Without home-built locomotives, however, Californians relied on eastern manufacturers. Like the early English-built locomotives shipped to America, these East Coast locomotives were knocked down in pieces and loaded on ships bound for San Francisco.

Among the most famous of these 4-4-0 American class eastern imports, was the *Gov. Stanford* Built in 1862 by the Norris Works of Philadelphia, it worked on the construction of the transcontinental railroad. The engine was named for Leland Stanford, wealthy merchant, California governor and one of the "Big 4" who financed and built the transcontinental railroad from the West. Looking for cheap and reliable labor, Stanford recruited thousands of "coolies" from China to hand-build the most treacherous part of the line across the High Sierras.

Left:
The elegant but essential cowcatcher on the "Gov. Stanford" locomotive cleared the tracks of errant steers, as well as bears and other wildlife.

Opposite:
Central Pacific No. 1 was named for railroad promoter and California governor, Leland Stanford. On loan from Stanford University, the engine is displayed at the California State Railroad Museum. Stanford's great wealth built Stanford University.

Photographed at the California State Railroad Museum, Sacramento, CA

Western Riches...

Mining and Railroading

Mining has long enriched American railroads. Coal is so vital to railroads that it's been dubbed "King Coal" or "Black Diamonds." Today, coal trains operate in conveyor-like fashion from Wyoming's Powder River mines to power plants nationwide.

Back in the 1860s and 1870s, it was silver that gave railroads their first taste of fabulous mineral riches. Nevada's Comstock Lode generated so much profit that the Virginia & Truckee Railroad (V&T) could have laid its rails in silver. Linking the transcontinental Central Pacific line to Virginia City, Nevada, short line V&T made ten million dollars a month in today's dollars. It hauled in supplies, passengers and prospectors, and hauled out silver ore and new millionaires. Some of this profit flowed into the Central Pacific through its V&T junction.

Above:
The sand dome, brass bell and steam pump sit proudly atop the boiler of No. 21, the "J. W. Bowker."

Right:
The brass builder's plate on the J. W. Bowker smoke chest shows the V&T Nevada engine was made in Philadelphia by Baldwin in 1875.

The brass-trimmed J.W.Bowker was a wood-burning locomotive as evidenced by its large, balloon smokestack. It also featured a huge steam water pump atop the boiler for fire fighting. Eventually retired, the engine rode to glory in 1939 in Cecil B. DeMille's epic motion picture *Union Pacific,* and it has also appeared in many other more recent films. Although owned by the Nevada State Railroad Museum, the engine is displayed in Sacramento.

Flaunting It...

1875 Virginia & Truckee Railroad No. 13 *Empire*

No. 13, a freight engine from the Virginia & Truckee Railroad, reflects railroad wealth and fancy decorative ornamentation. Locomotive ornamentation began in the 1840s, driven by pride and the advent of color lithography, which encouraged builders to advertise a showy product.

Boilers were wrapped in a polished, silver-blue sheet metal known as "Russia Iron." Fittings were brass, cabs were of finished walnut, cherry or oak. With its gold leaf, gleaming brass, and red wheels, No. 13 flaunted high fashion.

Steam locomotives were fueled by wood until the later half of the 1800s. By some estimates over a million acres of American forest were consumed by fireboxes before the switch over to coal. Coal soot and smoke, which blackened engines, were the death knell of ornamentation. Thereafter, most locomotives were painted black.

Above:
Fine gold leaf scrollwork and red detailing elevate No. 13's sand dome to a work of art.

Right:
The showy No. 13 was a new, more powerful class of steam locomotive with 3 pairs of driving wheels. Known as a Mogul, this 2-6-0 class was produced into the 20th century.

Above:
The rolling opulence of No. 13 extends to the tender and even its wheels. Here, and on previous pages, the engine is reflected in a wall of mirrors at the California State Railroad Museum in Sacramento.

First Cousin of Thomas!

The Kahuku...1890 0-4-2T

Saddle tank engines were popular on plantations where clearances were tight but grades relatively modest. Like the famous *Thomas the Tank Engine*, the Kahuku 0-4-2T steam locomotive, carried its water supply in a donut-like saddle over the boiler. Unlike the fictional *Thomas* of England, the Kahuku spent its working life on the Kahuku Sugar Cane Plantation on the Hawaiian island of Oahu.

To make these work-a-day saddle tank engines as compact as possible, and to add extra weight over the driving wheels, water and fuel were carried aboard the engine itself, with no tender.

The Kahuku is owned by the Roaring Camp Railroads and is still operational. However, its side-rod piston drive is ill suited to steep grades.

Opposite page:
Framed by the cab front, the brass bell, steam whistle, sand and steam domes are all shown in this shot of the Hawaiian saddle tank engine, "Kahuku."

Photographed at the Roaring Camp Railroads, Felton, CA

Above left:
The diminutive Kahuku No. 3 worked half a century on a narrow gauge sugar plantation railroad.

Above right:
With no tender, saddle tank engines carried fuel and water aboard the locomotive.

Small Engines, Big Power...

**Heisler No. 2 Tuolumne
(1899, ex-West Side Lumber Co.
No. 3, Tuolumne, CA)**

Hardworking geared locomotives were employed in the East as well as the West and South. They were in their element wherever flimsy track, steep grades or tight curves conspired to trip up standard, side-rod steam engines.

Geared locomotives were common on narrow gauge lines where rails were 36 inches apart or smaller. Some also worked the larger standard gauge of 4 feet, 8.5 inches.

This Tuolumne No. 2 Heisler engine was built in 1899 by Stearns of Erie, Pennsylvania. Unlike Shay engines, the Heisler locomotives featured a center drive shaft with power to a geared axle in each two-axle wheel truck. Side rods powered the other axle. This combination enabled the Heisler to achieve greater speed, while retaining its ability to climb grades.

Photographed at the Roaring Camp Railroads, Felton, CA

Geared Up...

Ohio Roots, Southern Service, Eastern Preservation

The large, three-truck, geared Shay pictured here has a checkered history. Displayed at the Railroad Museum of Pennsylvania in Strasburg, the standard gauge engine was built in 1906 by Lima Locomotive Works of Ohio. From there it traveled to Enterprise Lumber Co. in Sims, Louisiana, where it hauled logs for many years. After its sale to the Ely-Thomas Lumber Company, the locomotive served out the remainder of its working years in Fenwick, West Virginia.

Still operable in 1965, it was rescued by the Strasburg Rail Road. The Strasburg then sent the engine across the street to the Railroad Museum. Today it is part of a world-class collection of steam, electric and diesel engines preserved in a massive, 100,000-square-foot train hall.

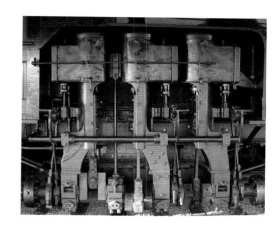

Above:

The vertical cylinders of a 3-piston Shay power an exterior drive shaft geared to the steam locomotive's axles.

Left:

This big, wood-burning Shay is preserved by the Railroad Museum of Pennsylvania in Strasburg.

Photographed at the Railroad Museum of Pennsylvania, Strasburg, PA

Opposite:

The brute strength and power of the geared Shay locomotive can't be overstated.

From Yard Goat to Museum Piece...

On the Mend!

With over a century to its credit, No. 1187 is ready for an overhaul. Built in 1903, the 0-4-0 steam switch engine was towed into the shops at the Railroad Museum of Pennsylvania in 2006 for a potential rebuild.

The camelback style switcher has a center cab designed to give engineer and fireman a doubled-ended view when shunting cars around rail yards. The jury is still out on the fate of No. 1187. Depending on the condition of its boiler plates it will be restored to full operation or cosmetically refurbished only. Steam preservation is an ongoing labor of love for non-profit organizations. Full restoration for this locomotive, even with the aid of volunteers, could easily exceed $100,000.00.

Opposite page:
In its dilapidated state, it's hard to believe No. 1187 arrived under its own power at the Strasburg Rail Road in Pennsylvania. But that was nearly a half century ago and the engine is now slated for overhaul.

Above:
Basking in the late afternoon sun, No. 1187 and a trail of cars cut an impressive silhouette on the grounds of the Railroad Museum of Pennsylvania at Strasburg.

"Some Say You're Born with It"

A 21st century engineer running both steam locomotives and diesel engines is a rarity. The old engineers who made the transition from steam to diesel in the 1940s and '50s are long gone. There are, however, a handful of professional railroaders who so admire the grit and glory of yesteryear, that they volunteer countless weekends to run big steam. Bill Wilson, 54, of Lansing, Michigan is one of them.

By day, and sometimes night, Wilson is a diesel engineer for Norfolk Southern, often cited as the best-run freight railroad in America. On weekends, he takes the throttle of the big 2-8-4 Berkshire steam locomotive at the Steam Railroading Institute, in Owosso, Michigan. "The biggest challenge of running a steam engine is knowing how to set the cutoff or reverse bar or wheel," says Wilson. Often called a "Johnson Bar," the reverse bar controls both direction and valve timing. "Depending on the number of cars and your speed, if you don't set it properly you could almost tear the engine to pieces," adds Wilson. "It's a little bit like a manual transmission in a car." Imagine merging into high-speed interstate traffic in first gear and you get an idea of the havoc an inexperienced engineer can inflict on a 400-ton steam locomotive.

"In a diesel engine you've just got forward, neutral and reverse. The controls are more compact, grouped and automated," Wilson observes. On a steam engine the controls are manual, the job physically exhausting, the finesse exacting. "Some say you're born with it, some say you're not. I probably put in 20 hours every weekend in the summer" at SRI, says Wilson. "But I don't do one-tenth of the work that goes on there." Wilson grew up around trains. Like many railroaders, he followed his father, an engineer for the New York Central, into the profession as a teenager.

Long Life on Short Lines!

1916 Baldwin 2-8-0 Consolidation

An outgrowth of the smaller and earlier Atlantic and Mogul engines, the 2-8-0 Consolidation class was not named for its new wheel arrangement. Rather this advance in steam locomotive technology coincided with the consolidation of several regional eastern lines into the Lehigh Valley system.

The first of these locomotives were built by the Lehigh and quickly proved their mettle as good runners. When other railroads embraced the 2-8-0, the Consolidation moniker came with it. No. 15 was manufactured by Baldwin Locomotive works in 1916. This Consolidation lugged lumber and coal in the Tennessee hill country as No. 20 for the Oneida & Western Railroad. After migrating north to Rahway Valley Railroad of New Jersey, it was renumbered.

Over 23,000 Consolidations were turned out by various locomotive makers. The engine eventually gave way to bigger and faster locomotives. Its relatively small boiler, and small drivers were incapable of providing the great speed and stamina demanded by big 20th century railroads.

Above:

The Consolidation's 2-8-0 wheel arrangement was an important advance in railroad technology. The large rectangular shape under the cab and part of the boiler, is the engine's firebox.

105

This One's a Keeper...

1929 Baldwin 0-6-0 Switching Locomotive

When you care enough to build the very best—keep it for yourself. That apparently was the philosophy of Baldwin Locomotive Works when it built this versatile 0-6-0 steam switcher. The slope-backed tender of efficient No. 26 promised maximum visibility for the crew. It also helped ensure this switcher would live on.

Built in 1929 on the eve of the stock market crash and the Great Depression, No. 26 was retained by Baldwin to work its sprawling fabricating plant in Eddystone, Pennnsylvania. Baldwin was one of the top steam locomotive manufacturers, along with Lima of Ohio, and ALCO of Schenectady, NY. Baldwin survived the change from steam to diesel, producing the distinctive "shark nose diesels." Ultimately it bit the bullet, surrendering to the Generals of the locomotive makers—General Motors and General Electric.

Opposite:
The slide rod valves of No. 2, Baldwin switcher 0-6-0, are etched by the late afternoon light.

Below:
No. 26 was prized. It was kept by its maker to switch the huge Baldwin Locomotive complex at Eddystone, Pennsylvania.

Photographed at Steamtown National Historic Site, Scranton, PA

Above:
The squat appearance of a Porter Tank Engine belies the power that made these tank engines vital to industrial America.

1930 Porter 0-6-0

Rechargeable engines were captives, both to their owners and their inability to generate steam. Squat, rotund and charming in appearance, these little locomotives were indentured to their industrial owners.

Known as rechargeable engines, they were also dubbed "fireless" locomotives or "fireless cookers" because they had no firebox and no fuel. Instead, they had a large "tank" in place of the standard boiler. The tank was pumped up or charged with a shot of steam from the factory boilers at the beginning of the day. The Porters kept running until the diminishing steam pressure in the boiler failed to drive the pistons. At which point they were recharged. Since they were tied to a stationary source of steam, they never strayed far.

Below left:
The builders plate identifies this locomotive as an H.K. Porter product from Pittsburgh built in 1930.

Below right:
The compact versatility of the H.K. Porter tank engines made them indispensable to factories, foundries, steel and brass mills from Waterbury, CT to Birmingham, AL.

Photographed at the Wanamaker, Kempton and Southern Railroad, Kempton, PA

Above:
For an industrial switch engine, "D" shows off an art deco livery rivaling streamlined passenger locomotives.

Photographed at the Railroad Museum of Pennsylvania, Strasburg, PA

The World's Largest "Fireless-Cooker"

So impressive was this Heisler Fireless locomotive that it made its debut on the world stage at the 1939–40 New York World's Fair. It captivated crowds looking for the first or biggest of anything on display. In fact, this "fireless cooker" locomotive without a firebox, qualified in at least two categories. At 100,000 lbs., it was the largest rechargeable locomotive ever, and the first and only engine of its type to have eight driving wheels.

The 0-8-0 was also, no doubt, the first and only industrial switch engine to show up at a World's Fair sporting a teal blue, art deco design. After the World's Fair the engine went to work for a paper company in Erie, PA. Later it served a 30-year stint at a steam power plant lugging and shunting coal cars. The plant designated its engines with letters. The locomotive was cosmetically restored to its World's Fair appearance by the Railroad Museum of Pennsylvania.

Boy, Oh Boy! ...

1940 Union Pacific No. 4012, Alco 4-8-8-4

The steam locomotive grew ever larger even as diesel engines were starting to make inroads. It reached gargantuan proportions with the Union Pacific Railroad's legendary "Big Boys." Only 25 Big Boy engines were built, but they were monsters. Each weighed one million, two hundred thousand pounds. They stretched nearly to the 50-yard line of a football field.

The 4-8-8-4 locomotives were actually two engines in one. Behind the cowcatcher and pilot wheels was a massive pair of cylinders and side rods powering eight driving wheels. Right behind the first set of drivers was another matching pair of big cylinders and eight more driving wheels. A trailing truck supported the cavernous coal-burning firebox and cab. Attached to the Big Boy was a 14-wheeled "centipede" tender that held 56,000 lbs. of coal and 25,000 gallons of water.

Built by Alco, these behemoths were designed to pull 150 car freights through the Wyoming-Utah Wasatch Mountains without helper engines. This was something that the Big Boys did with ease. Although built for power and traction, not speed, these remarkable engines were capable of 80 mph. Still in their youth, the last of the Big Boys were retired in the 1950s. Six are preserved, but none are operable.

Photographed at Steamtown National Historic Site, Scranton, PA

Above:
The Big Boy was also a cover boy! One of these mighty engines once made the cover of TIME magazine.

Chapter Five:
The Back Shop...

The ongoing task of repairing and maintaining locomotives was performed at railroad back shops that seem quaint and primitive in hindsight. Before the widespread introduction of electric motors, electro-magnets and hydraulics, human muscle did most of the brute work.

In larger or more modern shops, stationary steam locomotives supplemented brawn. The blacksmith was king of the early back shop. He hand-forged or molded most of the replacement parts needed to restore ailing steam engines. This scene from the early roundhouse and shops at California's Railtown 1897 State Historic Park, shows the forge and many of the elements essential to railroad blacksmithing. Railtown is a favorite setting for Hollywood Westerns that feature early steam locomotives.

Letting Off Steam...

Mongrel Locomotives!

In addition to routine maintenance and back shop overhaul, larger and more progressive railroads were constantly tinkering with the efficiency of factory-made locomotives. New parts and whole assemblies were grafted on to factory-built engines. Because terrain, operating conditions and traffic varied greatly between railroads, customization was especially appealing.

But, local modifications, updates and improvements resulted in thousands of locomotive mutts, with no two exactly alike. This development accelerated steam's downfall. When confronted with the uniform, mass-produced, easy-to-repair diesel engines with their interchangeable parts, the customized steam locomotive was glaringly expensive to maintain and hopelessly outmoded. The comparison was so dramatic; many newly made steam engines went under the junkyard torch in their infancy.

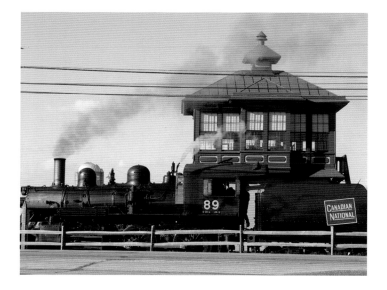

Left:

Bell clanging, a train nears the station. Canadian engines like this one outlived those in the States. Thus, operating engines today are often Canadian, including a popular locomotive at Strasburg Railroad in Pennsylvania.

Opposite page:

Double Header!
In a cloud of smoke and steam, two locomotives head up a mountain grade. For traction, sand is fed to the wheels from a boiler dome.

Below:

Watch Out!
Expelling condensed water from the cylinders, a cloud
of steam and scalding water shoots down the
engineer's side of a locomotive at New Hope,
Pennsylvania.

Homegrown

Advances in technology, coupled with modern shops staffed by highly skilled craftsmen, led many big railroads to began fabricating new locomotives from scratch. During the first half of the 20th century thousands of home-built locomotives were produced. At the Juniata Works in Altoona, the Pennsylvania Railroad built more of its own locomotives than any other railroad. And, unlike other railroads, the Pennsylvania Railroad prized standardization.

A few hundred miles south in Roanoke, Virginia, the headquarter's shops of the Norfolk & Western Railway (N&W) produced the most advanced and efficient locomotives in the world. Construction there continued into the 1950s. Sadly, even these beautifully engineered steam locomotives could not withstand the diesel onslaught. Norfolk & Western earned millions of dollars annually hauling coal from the mines of the Virginias for both export and domestic consumption. Loyal to its revenue-producing customers, N&W was the last bastion of big, mainline steam, before throwing in the towel in the late 1950s.

Below left:

Cylinders, valves, whistles, leaks and stacks all emit the precious steam that drives locomotives. Here, steam escapes from the top of the slide valves that regulate steam to the cylinders.

Below right:

Poised to let loose with steam's romantic calling card, the whistle on a boiler dome stands at the ready! In the old days, engineers were recognized solely by the distinctive wail of their whistles.

Left:

*Linked to other drivers by a rod
and pin, the rear driving wheel
is stopped by an airbrake at
lower left. The small pipe just
above the rail is a sander.*

Right:

*A relief valve exhales steam
below the boiler.*

Below:

Steam floats through valves and pipes from the cab and down the long
boiler. The fascinating mechanics of a steam engine are exposed,
adding to their magical appeal.

Overleaf:

Taking a breather, an idling locomotive blows off steam. During
station stops, engines with well-stoked fires build up steam pressure
rapidly. Safety valves on the far left-dome will be popping off steam if
the engine does not move soon.

Working on the Railroad...

An Army 2 Million Strong!

Work on the railroad was often compared to military life. At the turn of the 19th century, two million Americans toiled in hundreds of different railroad crafts, from hoggers and hostlers to car knockers, boomers and gandy dancers

Because danger was a constant companion and attention imperative, a rulebook governed every job—on and off the train. A rigid hierarchy and harsh discipline enforced train orders and regulations to the letter.

The elite who rode express passenger trains manned the front lines. In addition to the engine crew, their ranks included conductors, dining car stewards, chefs, Pullman porters and bartenders. Premium trains offered barbers, nurses and even private secretaries.

All shared in the glory and hazards of working on *Limiteds*, *Chiefs*, *Super Chiefs* and *Rockets*. Express passenger trains, and fast time freights that made railroads rich, were the pinnacle of prestige.

All Aboard!

Although the engineer was heroic, the conductor was the boss of the train. Often addressed as "Captain," he was responsible for the welfare of passengers and tickets, fares, bookkeeping and timekeeping. A train couldn't move until the conductor signaled the engineer and uttered his two-word command, "ALL ABOARD!" As befitting his high station, an old-time conductor wore a brass-buttoned suit, watch-pocket vest, starched shirt, tie and billed cap. Rulebooks spelled out the dress code.

Below left:

Walking his train before giving the "All Aboard," the conductor or train "Captain," gives orders—even to the engineer.

Opposite page:

Looking like the "Singing Brakeman," legendary 1920s country singer Jimmie Rodgers, an East Broad Top Railroad trainman perches on steps flanking the car vestibule. Railroad songs have always captured the imagination, from "City of New Orleans" to "Wabash Cannonball."

In Harm's Way

Inside the cab of a racing steam locomotive, danger and sometimes death rode with engineer and fireman. Balanced precariously between the engine cab and the coal tender, the fireman stoked a 2,500-degree inferno raging in the giant firebox.

Squinting through clouds of rushing steam, smoke and cinders, and nearly blind-sided by the long boiler, the engineer strained to see rails and signals ahead. It was akin to looking down the side of a huge cannon, eyes wide for washouts, cars, cows and other trains.

The celebrated Casey Jones missed a flag signal in 1900 when he careened into the back of a standing freight train at Vaughn, Mississippi. But unlucky engineers and firemen could also die in derailments, landslides or bridge collapses. Others were scalded or instantly vaporized when locomotive boilers exploded.

Running a steam locomotive was as much an art as a skill. A good "hogger" or engineer ran at speed, expending coal and water like a miser. A 100-car train, upwards of a mile long, was often strung out over hills and valleys. Keeping it from breaking apart took a steady throttle hand and deft touch of the air brakes.

Above:

*A fireman looks backward down the train for a
switchman's signal. When moving, firemen balance
on a steel plate between engine and tender, shoveling
coal to the firebox. Exposed to the elements and the
pitching of the locomotive, firemen are in a
precarious position.*

127

Above:

"Steel-drivin' man" swinging a maul, the trackman drives home steel spikes that hold the rail to wooden ties or "sleepers." This trackman has just replaced a sleeper. He straddles a track jack for lifting rails.

Keeping Track

The choreographed motion of maul-swinging spike drivers and trackmen gave rise to the colorful "gandy dancer" moniker. Romanced in song, *John Henry, the steel drivin' man,* added luster to otherwise brutal, backbreaking work of building railroads by hand.

Maintenance was constant. The steam engine's pounding side rods and massive driving wheels assaulted the rails, cracking steel, prying out spikes and loosening rails. On curves, trains spread rails out of gauge. If not spotted and repaired, derailments followed.

Right:

A small inspection car or track speedster carries a crew of two. Speedsters are the descendents of old hand cars, pumped by two men flanking a fulcrum in the middle of the car

Below:

A trackman's tools are from left: tie tongs, track gauge rod, maul, and rail pullers to winch rails into proper gauge.

Yard Work

In perilous freight yards, the number of missing fingers testified to years of service. In a bruising, ear-jarring process little changed today, cars are banged, humped, switched, shoved and sorted. "Cuts" of cars bound for the same destination are marshaled into trains.

Above:

Before rolling into the round-house, a locomotive pauses on the lip of a turntable. The trainman rakes coal ash and "clinkers" from the firebox grate into the ash pan.

Opposite page:

A trainman hoses down the hot ash pan. Cooling off the ashes before dumping, guards against fires that can incinerate round-houses.

Brakemen hang off ladders on rolling freight cars or, in the old days, ran across car roofs, jumping from car to car. When a car is moving too fast, the brakeman applies hand brakes. Just before the car slams into and couples to other cars, he jumps off. If cars fail to couple, an engine nudges them together. In the Steam Age before radios, fingers, hands and feet were severed when brakeman and engineer got their signals crossed.

Busy yards today have parallel tracks with constant traffic. One misstep and brakemen or switchmen can be cut down by a 250-ton, free-rolling car.

Down by the Station

In small stations on busy lines, station agents juggled multiple jobs—selling tickets, processing freight and dispatching train orders. In big terminals like New York's Grand Central or Chicago's Union Station, the agent managed hundreds of workers.

For a century the telegraph and telephone were the primary means of communication. In most stations, a telegrapher or "brass pounder" served with the agent.

In the meantime, the railroads' autocratic structure spawned the American labor movement in the 19th century. As a result, then and even now, railroaders are among the best-paid workers in America.

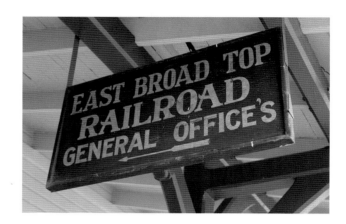

Above:

This sign at the East Broad Top Railroad points to the general offices, home of the "railroad brass."

Right:

An old hand-pulled baggage cart is loaded with bags and freight tossed from the baggage car door.

Photographed at the Railroad Museum of Pennsylvania, Strasburg, PA

Above:

The station agent raises the window when selling tickets. Behind the closed window, the agent tends the books between trains. Until Amtrak in 1972, ticket agents made reservations using racks of timetables from dozens of American and Canadian railroads. This preserved waiting room is at the WK&S line in Kempton, PA.

Chapter Six: Mountain High...

An alluring escape from the paved-over orchards, parking lots and factories of California's Silicon Valley awaits the adventurer in the coastal mountains just west of the Bay Area. Many steam railroads that are geared toward families and tourists are situated in the seemingly remote or untouched countryside, adding greatly to their appeal. This railroad is no exception. Here a teakettle Shay locomotive plugs up a mountain grade in Felton. The cool mountain air of summer wafts clouds of steam vapor into the forest. A thousand feet below on the valley floor temperatures soar into the 90s.

From Arizona's busy Grand Canyon Railroad to the jaw-dropping route of the Cumbres & Toltec Scenic Railway in New Mexico and Colorado, tourist lines have been embraced by the public. A nostalgic yearning for times past contributes to their popularity. But the steam locomotive itself is the real draw.

All pictures in this chapter photographed at the Roaring Camp Railroads, Felton, CA

Above:
Morning mists from redwood forests bathe the engine house at the Roaring Camp Railroads in Felton, California.

Conquering the Toughest Terrain!

The world's oldest and tallest trees share the mountains with venerable logging locomotives at Roaring Camp and Big Trees Narrow Gauge Railroad. Deep in the coastal redwoods of the Santa Cruz Mountains near San Francisco, this steep and scenic narrow gauge railroad has a roster of seven engines. Most are geared steam locomotives, built for the twisting tracks and tortuous terrain of rugged logging and mining operations.

Geared locomotives are powerful, but plodding. Tortoise-like speeds, often below 10 mph, are the norm. What they lack in speed, however, these locomotives make up for in tenacity—clawing their way up mountainsides, while clinging to hairpin curves. A grade or hill of more than 2% on mainline railroads is considered steep, often calling for pusher engines and double—or triple-headers. By contrast, the steepest grade on the Roaring Camp line up Bear Mountain is over 4 times greater, at 8.5%.

For a truck or car driving up an 8.5% hill (an incline of 8.5 feet in 100 feet of distance), it's a simple matter of downshifting. For conventional steam or diesel engines hauling long, heavy loads, this climb is impossible.

To surmount the steep, twisting grades of 19th century narrow gauge railroads, the geared locomotive was developed in 1872. Most were "Shays" named after inventor, Ephraim Shay. These steam locomotives feature vertical cylinders and a geared outside drive. With cylinders on the right side and an offset boiler on the left, the odd-looking Shay is lopsided, but perfectly suited for the job.

Left:

Climbing aboard a Roaring Camp narrow gauge diesel switcher, an engineer starts his day in the dripping mountain fog.

Right:

The Dixiana Steam Shay, pride of the railroad, emerges from the engine house for another day of work.

Firing Up and Bottling Up

The antique geared engines that survive at Roaring Camp all burn oil. That calls for a unique "firing up" ritual, unlike anything at a coal-fired railroad.

When coal-fired steam engines are "put to bed," hot firebox coals are banked, or shoved together. Like the coal furnaces that heated American homes until the 1950s, the banked coals glow for hours, maintaining sufficient steam in the boiler to keep home radiators warm or fire up locomotives at dawn. But oil is either on or off. There are no coals to bank. So, the crew of a Shay engine "bottles up" the locomotive for the night. The fire is extinguished. After water temperature in the boiler drops below boiling, valves are shut to preserve, or "bottle up," the heat.

At dawn the boiler is still warm, but without steam to vaporize or atomize oil and spray it over the firebox. So, a jet of flaming natural gas replaces the oil spray, gradually raising the temperature in the firebox. Once there is enough heat to generate steam, natural gas is shut off and the steam-driven oil spray is turned on full blast. Soon, the engine is fired up and ready to roll.

Every year, throngs of tourists ride the popular Roaring Camp trains, taking in the towering splendor of the redwoods. The ancient stand of redwoods enveloping the railroad was the first to be protected in America over a century ago.

Left:

Oil cans, to lubricate the many bearings of a Shay, sit next to the pot-like fuel lid on the engine's tender. The pipe behind the lid carries water to the coiled fire hose, which is also mounted on the tender.

Right:

A fireman displays a diagram of the locomotive firebox and boiler tubes that vent the firebox and generate steam in the water-filled boiler.

Left:
Adjusting the flow of water and oil, a fireman prepares to depart. The firebox door is to his right.

Rolling Thunder!

Blasting out of the engine house with a full head of steam, the Dixiana prepares to assault the tough grade up Bear Mountain. Sometimes likened to overgrown teakettles, Shays provide big power on a minimum of steam.

In its 3-mile plus roundtrip up Bear Mountain, the Shay will burn 100 gallons of fuel and expend 500 gallons of water. By comparison, the railroad's diesel makes the trip on five gallons of fuel and no water.

What the Dixiana lacks in efficiency, it makes up for in drama. The engine is geared down for maximum traction and minimum speed. The furious pumping and gasping of pistons highlights the mighty struggle to overcome gravity. Accentuated by hissing steam, whistle blasts, burning oil, and smoke, the complex mechanism is totally exposed. In sober contrast, the diesel's inner workings are concealed. Its monotonous drone is efficient, but uninspiring. Steam and smoke are gone, and the diesel horn is flat and dull.

The Lima Locomotive Works of Ohio built the Dixiana in 1912. It earned the Dixie moniker after working for a now abandoned mining operation in Dixiana, Virginia. The engine's historic significance is recognized by its designation as a "National Mechanical Engineering Historic Landmark."

Above:
The Dixiana Shay blows off a swirl of steam, blasting out of the safety valves and billowing from its cylinders.

Left:
Engineer and brakeman inspect the vertical cylinders and geared drive of the Shay locomotive.

Left:
Framed by huge redwoods, the Dixiana Shay pulls its train of yellow cars through a sharp bend on a mountain trestle. The basket atop the smoke stack is a spark arrestor.

Overleaf:
Positioned in the trestle timbers just below the thundering locomotive, the photographer contrasts the bold drama of industrial might with the play of sun on nature's oldest trees.

Chapter Seven:
Rolling Stock...

An engine without a train is really not a train at all. In railroad jargon a moving locomotive with nothing to pull is "deadheading." The term is also applied to passengers traveling for free on a company pass. In either case, it illustrates the importance of revenue generating freight and passengers. Rolling stock is the generic term applied to the moneymaking freight and passenger cars of a train.

There are hundreds of specialized freight cars varying greatly in size and shape. But most fit into six basic groups: boxcar, flatcar, stock car (primarily for cattle), gondola, hopper and tanker. The surge in global trade has created the new and highly profitable "well car." These cars can transport a moving mountain of containers, one stacked upon another in towering blocks. But well cars, or stack cars, were unknown in the Steam Age. More typical is the dilapidated, steel-braced, wood sheathed car shown at left. It probably started life as a heavy-duty, flatcar. Then it morphed into a track gang car, before discarded and forgotten on a rusty spur.

Cash and Carry!...

Boxcars, an American Invention!

Freight has always been the mainstay of railroading. The first steam trains served mines and quarries. While passengers took to the rails quickly, they were often conveyed in "mixed trains" of both freight and passenger cars. Old engravings show barrels and freight stacked on flatcars, or atop stage-like passenger cars.

Little more than open wagons, early freight cars were imported from England. The harsh North American weather soon led to an American innovation—the covered boxcar. Boxcars protected shipments from the elements and, not incidentally, they allowed railroads to demand more cash for carrying covered freight.

Along with rougher weather, early American track and roadbeds were also rough. To keep cars from derailing, Americans invented doubled-axle trucks on a swiveling bolster attached to the underside of the car. With two trucks to a boxcar and a combined total of eight wheels, these flexible trucks kept cars on the rails. They also permitted much larger, longer and heavier cars than the rigid, 4-wheeled English counterparts.

Below:
A turn of the century West Coast boxcar shows the double-axle swivel trucks that enabled American cars to haul much heavier loads.

Opposite page:
The corner of a wooden, steel-braced boxcar shows the brakeman's ladder rails on one side, the hand brake wheel on the other. All freight cars have both air and hand brakes.

In John Steinbeck's *East of Eden* classic, the Trask family loses everything when their lettuce spoils on a Southern Pacific freight train. By the time refrigerator cars, or iced reefers, like these were in common usage, spoilage was rare. Western lines recognized the fortune to be made shipping fresh California fruit and produce to hungry eastern markets.

Wood-sheathed reefers from the Fruit Growers Express had ice compartments, or bunkers, on each end. Before fresh fruit or vegetables were loaded, the cars were "iced down." Heavy lidded hatches at the top ends of the cars were opened. Using long, steel-tipped rods, trainmen then maneuvered enormous blocks of ice into the reefer's bunkers, keeping the car's contents cool and crisp on the way East.

Above and left:
Specialty boxcars included these reefers from Fruit Growers Express. Fruit and produce reefers were chilled by enormous blocks of ice.

Opposite page:
A wooden boxcar brings up the tail end of a string of cars. The ubiquitous brownish paint on boxcars then and now is known as "boxcar red."

Bulk Shipping, Backbone of the Railroad

Heavy or bulky commodities are the backbone of most railroad operations. Back in the 1860s when railroads pushed onto the plains where trees were rare, coal replaced wood in steam engine fireboxes. Railroads became the mines' best customers, along with iron and steel mills, factories, power plants and home furnaces.

Back then, and even today, railroads had huge fleets of high-walled open hoppers or gondolas to ship coal and other minerals from mine to market. Both ends of each hopper car were sloped or steeply inclined. This design promoted rapid discharge of coal when the bottom hatches were opened. About 40% of all railroad revenue continues to be from coal. Much of it is still hauled in hoppers with bottom hatches. Unit trains made up of aluminum "Bathtub" gondolas are making inroads on the traditional hoppers. These bathtub gons can be rotated 180 degrees and dumped from the top.

Above:
The sloping sides of coal hoppers are clearly visible here. The cars are linked by inter-locking steel couplers. The hose at right is the air brake line.

Oil to Orange Juice

The first tank cars were nothing more than barrels turned on end. Liquid contents were often molasses or whale oil. After the Civil War, the emerging petroleum industry created an ever-increasing demand for tankers. Although dozens of designs exist today for hauling ever-larger quantities of everything from liquefied natural gas to orange juice, the basic concept remains unchanged.

Most tank cars are filled from the top. Traditional tankers have an expansion dome, plus safety valves to release pressure that can build up in shipment. If not vented, increasing pressure can cause leaks or even explode the car. Tankers are generally unloaded from another set of valves in the belly of the car.

Left:
Tank cars are filled from the top and emptied from the belly.

Super-Sizing

Common tank cars were 28 feet long with riveted seams. The tanks were mounted on rigid steel frames, and generally carried up to 8,000 gallons. The widespread use of automobiles and the pressing demand for petroleum products, especially during and after World War II, led to huge tank car fleets. These fleets were, and still are, owned by the oil companies.

Like most railroad cars from boxcars to lumber cars, tankers have been super-sized. Welded seam tankers without frames or domes have greatly increased capacity. Some chemical tankers carry over 40,000 gallons. Glass lined tankers haul a huge array of liquid foodstuffs, from beer to salad oil and corn syrup.

Above:
This steam-era tanker carried hazardous material, as indicated by the red placards on the front and side.

Above:
Two old, wood-sided gondolas snooze in the
early morning. Time has robbed the skeletal
left car of its wooden sides. But the air brake
hose between the cars appears new.

Back to the Basics

The most utilitarian of all cars, the open gondola carries any heavy load that doesn't need to be shielded from the elements. The basic gondola is little more than a flatcar with low sides. It's been the railroad's heavy-duty best friend since 1870. Pig iron, coal, steel, sand, scrap, bailed aluminum, girders, rocks, railroad ties, concrete barriers, pipes, and telephone poles—you name it, and the gondola has hauled it. The gondola has changed little in a hundred years. Steel has replaced wood siding. Hinged, drop-down ends and deeper "fish belly" sides allow for longer or heavier loads. Some gondolas even have enormous steel lids to protect finished steel and other polished, metal goods. Although widespread throughout the nation, gondolas are easiest to spot around mills and junkyards.

Above and left:
The D&H logo on this gondola shows off a storied heritage. Built in 1907 for the Delaware & Hudson Railroad, it worked the bridge line to Montreal. The D&H is now part of the Canadian Pacific Railroad route to New York.

The Vanishing Exclamation Point!

When yesteryear's kids waited patiently, counting the cars of a passing freight, they were rewarded in the end. The star of every train has always been the powerful locomotive. By comparison, the colorful caboose served as the exclamation point of the train. It was humble, even cute, and definitely worth the wait. From his perch in the rooftop cupola, the conductor might beam a farewell. Other times, a brakeman on the caboose's back porch would wave a cheerful goodbye or swing a red lantern as the last car scurried down the tracks.

Opposite and below:

Sitting in the small rooftop cupola of a freight train caboose, the conductor watches for anything amiss on the rolling train.

The caboose was the freight conductor's castle. During the steam age and up to the 1990s, every freight had a caboose. In his small outpost 75 cars from the engine, the freight conductor tracked the train both on paper and by sight. He kept track of cars picked up or dropped off and processed bills of lading. High in the cupola, he surveyed the moving train. It was the conductor's job to spot a shifting load or smoking "hot box" wheel bearing that could break an axle and wreck the train. Alas, by the end of the 20th century, the loveable caboose had vanished. Its demise was a small computer mounted on the rear of the last freight car that performs the inspections once done by caboose crew.

Top:
On cold nights, a pot-belly stove warmed the cozy caboose. The stove top kept coffee and fried eggs hot in the morning.

Center:
The back door of the caboose opened to a small porch with steps on both sides.

Bottom:
Even the last car had hand brakes. From the side, the functional beauty of a simple brake wheel is apparent.

Opposite page:
A Reading Railroad caboose is permanently sidetracked.

Handcars and Speeders...

Above:
*A modern day, man-powered handcar sits on
a spur outside an engine house.*

Maintenance of Way

Railroads own their rights of way. Maintenance is a constant and costly job, generally without benefit of government subsidies or grants. In the 21st century, the army of trackmen and maintenance of way (MOW) workers generally ride trucks to the work site. But in the Steam Age, the MOW crew and trackmen went to work on a variety of small rail conveyances. These early vehicles were man-powered. Most were known as handcars because two men pumped the handles of a seesaw-like gear assembly that drove the wheels. Eventually handcars were motorized, not with small steam engines, but with lawnmower-like gasoline engines. Probably because they were faster than a handcar, these small motorized cars were dubbed "speedsters."

Above:
This brightly painted handcar is the simplest and smallest railroad vehicle. It's dwarfed by the engine axle behind it.

Below:
Speedsters are powerful enough to pull one or two MOW cars. In addition to track work, speedsters were once used as inspection cars.

Fire protection is paramount on railroads. Whether burning wood or coal, steam engines spewed sparks, hot ash, and embers. Although less frequent with diesel engines, the problem persists. Fires along endless rights-of-way are still frequent and sometimes costly, especially if they start prairie fires or burn bridges, ties, or nearby buildings. Railroads in every part of the nation are acutely aware of fire hazards. No more so than on logging lines or in the tinder-dry tall grass of the plains. To combat the problem, some steam locomotives on tourist lines carry fire hoses and steam driven pumps. On long trestles, sometimes MOW workers walk the line after every passing train. They look for hot embers that could lodge in the ties and set the bridge afire. As recently as the 1970s, the wood deck of the majestic New Haven Railroad Bridge across the Hudson River burned after it was set afire by a train pulled not by steam, but by diesel locomotives.

Above:
*This classy red fire truck saw years of service
fighting fires on western railroads. It is now
retired at the California State Railroad Museum
in Sacramento.*

Chapter Eight: Tracks to Everywhere...

Stand on a standard gauge track anywhere: a weedy Oregon spur or gleaming Delaware mainline. You're on a steel web spun across every state, from the remotest "burg" to the biggest city. At its apogee in 1916, the American steam railway system topped out at 254,000 miles. Abandonments have pruned back the total, but it's still vast.

In the East, traveling by train now is often a journey along littered tracks, through a forlorn landscape of tattered backyards and decaying factories. In the Steam Age, brick factories were prosperous, backyards tidy. Railroads tended to their property like the rich corporate titans they were. This chapter recalls the gilded age of rail-roading. In small towns and big cities, railway stations were the pride of the line. They flaunted wealth, power, and prestige. Coaling stations, water towers, signals, and even signposts were impeccably maintained.

Left:
The "clickety clack" of a train comes from wheels passing over joints like these between the rails. Jointed rails are bolted together with "fish plates."

Station Stop...

A Big Event in Small Town America

Stops on mainlines were infrequent, with most trains roaring by without slowing. On branch lines trains stopped, but there were far fewer of them. When a train approached, sleepy rural stations awoke in a hurry. Blasts from the steam whistle warned of the train's imminent arrival. As it rolled in, the conductor alighted, ready to shepard his passengers down the steep steps. Once all were off, the process was reversed. On long distance trains, boarding passengers was more involved, since the conductors assigned them to different cars based on their destinations.

On most trains, upfront baggage cars also carried parcels and priority shipments from the Railway Express Agency (REA). Heavy wood-planked baggage carts were dragged out to the train. Stacked high with baggage and parcels, these iron-wheeled carts were pulled by hand, their cargo muscled into the waiting baggage cars. If the train carried no mail car, mail sacks went with the baggage.

Opposite page:
Swathed in steam, a narrow gauge locomotive is fired up and ready to depart from a station on the East Broad Top Railroad.

Above:
Orbisonia Station snoozes during a lull between trains. In rural stations, the station agent and his family often lived on the upper floor.

Consolidations and Tex-Mex Steamers

Blasting condensed water from its cylinders, the New Hope & Ivyland Railway's 2-8-0 Baldwin locomotive marches out of New Hope, Pennsylvania in a cloud of steam. For nearly a half century, the railway has shuttled freight and tourists on a Bucks County branch of the old Reading Railroad.

The railroad's No. 40 is a Consolidation type locomotive built in 1925 in Philadelphia and sold to a South Carolina railroad for $25,125.96. It is the only operating steam locomotive on the New Hope & Ivyland Railroad. The for-profit railroad plans to supplement the Consolidation with a larger 4-8-4 refugee from Mexico repatriated to the United States nearly 40 years ago. Currently undergoing a complete overhaul, it is one of 32 light Northern engines fabricated by ALCO's Schenectady, New York shops for the National Railways of Mexico. In its prime, the locomotive hauled both fast freight and passengers between Mexico City and the Rio Grande River border at Laredo, Texas.

Opposite page:

In a scene reminiscent of the 1950s, No. 40 chugs out of New Hope's Victorian station with its distinctive "Witches' Hat" spiral dome. The telegrapher's office occupied the space under the dome.

Right:

An ancient iron-wheeled baggage cart displays autumn biennials outside the New Hope station.

Mixed Trains

On lightly used branch lines, or on main lines where passenger service wasn't a priority, steam railroads often ran mixed trains. Named for their mix of freight and passenger cars, these trains generally hauled a string of freight, mail or baggage cars up front, with one or two passenger cars tacked on the rear. Since speed and schedule were generally sacrificed to the laborious pickup and setout of freight or mail cars along the way, passengers often traveled at reduced fares. Mixed trains are nearly extinct on United States railroads. A few still survive on remote Canadian branches. Until recently Amtrak ran mixed diesel-powered trains on its Chicago-New York run over famed Horseshoe Curve through the Allegheny Mountains. These Amtrak trains put the passenger cars behind the engines for a smoother ride.A long string of material-handling cars made up the rear.

Left:
The freight house and station of the Wanamaker, Kempton & Southern Railroad is a beautiful example of a steam era country stop.

Above:
A later-day mixed train is ready for boarding at Kempton, Pennsylvania. The freight gondola behind the passenger coach offers open-air seating for tourists.

175

Above:
President Lincoln's steam train stopped at historic Hanover Junction in 1863 on its way to Gettysburg.

Footnote to History

A somber procession of Civil War hospital trains passed through this little-used junction in July 1863. They carried bleeding survivors of the Pennsylvania Battle of Gettysburg, turning point of the Civil War. Just four months later on Nov. 18, 1863, President Abraham Lincoln stopped here on his way to Gettysburg to dedicate the "hallowed ground" of a new national cemetery. A photo in the National Archives shows a towering Lincoln in top hat standing directly in front of the third window of this hotel/station. On the train, Lincoln polished his dedication speech, the Gettysburg Address.

The Civil War was the first test of steam trains in battle. At the start of the war at Bull Run, Virginia, Confederates rushed in reinforcements by rail, routed Union forces, and threatened Washington, D.C. As the war dragged on, Federal troops eventually sabotaged and disabled the Confederacy's railways. The South's major steam locomotive works in Richmond, Virginia, was also transformed into a munitions plant, further undermining the deteriorating system. Ironically, today the eastern rail network is dominated by the Norfolk Southern and CSX Railroads, both headquartered in the South.

Above:
The multi-story windows and porch balcony of Hanover Junction Station made this an impressive stopover when President Lincoln's special train paused here on its way from Washington to Gettysburg.

Left:
The clapboards, shutters and window frames attest to the meticulous restoration of this Civil War station hotel.

Rural Railroading...

Above:
The tail end of a train rounds a curve along a wooded right of way. This view of a caboose roof walk is from a window of the caboose's cupola.

Pick Up and Set Out

Local steam freights on country branches stopped every mile or so to pick up or set off loads and empties. Until trucks became common after World War I, nearly all shipments went by rail. Shippers or receivers of manufactured goods, grain, lumber, coal, or livestock were, by necessity, located on rail lines. To process everyday dispatch or receipt of freight cars, most passenger stations also had a nearby freight house.

Freight agents and their staff forwarded or accepted goods, billing shippers or collecting receipts for deliveries. Well into the 1950s, freight houses in small towns and big cities were vital to daily commerce. Families, farmers, and merchants picked up C.O.D. household appliances, birthday bicycles and other gifts, furniture, and seed. The Railway Express Agency, the rail equivalent of Federal Express, did a brisk business in parcels and packages. Early morning "milk trains" on lines reaching into big cities also stopped at dozens of country stations to pick-up the heavy, lidded cans brimming with the contents of the first milking.

Above:

Heavy-timbered, short-span bridges were the rule during the Steam Age. Even today with pre-stressed concrete and steel culverts, wood trestles are still common.

Right:

A typical branch line right of way is punctuated by a passing track and switch stand.

Below:

Diverging sidetracks split from the mainline like tree limbs in this view of a switchyard.

Signs and Signals

The first steam railroads needed neither signs nor signals. Speeds were relatively slow and the few stops were known to all. The need for signals was moot, since the first railroads had only one locomotive and few cars. As train traffic grew on the expanding system, so did signage and signals. Early signs were just placards announcing stations, yards, water and coal towers. Later, signage became ubiquitous. The most common were, and still are, number posts. These are vertical, black numbers on a waist-high white sign, concrete post or rock slab. They identify a location by measuring its distance from the origin of the line, usually a large city yard.

Early signals were displayed by trackside flagmen. They were also posted at busy road crossings. This practice continues even today on some hokey-pokey, lightly used branch lines without gates or flashing lights. Mechanized signals were first installed at stations. A series of metal balls suspended from a mast were raised or lowered by the station agent. A low ball meant stop; a highball, full steam ahead. Long after bladed signals and 3-color semaphores replaced the balls, the term "highball" was railroad argot for express train or fast freight with priority. A tall drink of mixed spirits and ice was also dubbed a "highball" after those signals. Modern railroads generally use alternating red, yellow and green lighted signals. These signs and signals are found at Kempton, Pennsylvania.

The bladed signal has both colored electric lights and a blade to indicate direction. This horizontal position and red light mean stop.

An old, raised iron sign functions as both caution for oncoming trains and a "No Trespassing" warning.

Trains overhang the width between rails by a couple of feet on each side. However, trackside structures sometimes narrow the right of way as indicated by this sign.

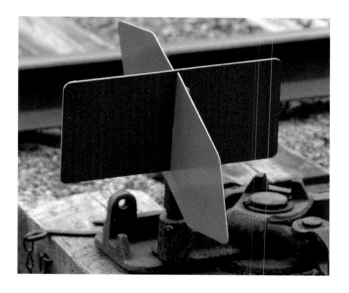

Switch signals indicate open or closed positions with red and green blades shown above or on the red arrow and white circle in the photograph on the facing page.

Wood, Steel, Coal

Three key components of the Steam Age supported and fueled locomotives. The great majority of railroad ties or sleepers are wood, generally soaked in a creosote preservative. The steel rails rest on the ties and, with help from crushed stone for drainage and ballast, they support passing trains. Depending on climate, maintenance, and traffic, wood ties can last upwards of 50 years. Railroads once marked the year of tie installation with large, numbered nails driven into the ties. Although these nails are sought after by souvenir hunters, they can still be found on some old lines. Until the advent of heavy, welded, mainline rail, rails came in 37-foot sections. The weight of the rail was measured in pounds per yard. On steam railroads, 90-pound rail was common. Today, 140 pounds or heavier is the norm on mainlines. Although sometimes fueled by wood and oil, most steam engines were fired by coal. Cinders and clinkers—rock hard, melted impurities in the coal—littered the roadbed. On poorly maintained lines, accumulated cinders and clinkers substituted for rock ballast.

Above:
Used ties are stacked and ready for sale to landscapers. Ties can last 50 years or more.

Left:
Sections of steel rail, known as stick rail, await installation on lightly used lines, sidings, or spurs.

Above:
The iron wheel of an old coal conveyor is framed by "black diamonds."

Powerful Thirst

When steam railroads built west, the line side structures they put up were often the first buildings in the area. Starting with the station, railroad architecture dominated both urban and rural landscape for a century. Since every steam engine had an unquenchable thirst, water towers were omnipresent. Nearly all had a hinged spout pulled down by the locomotive fireman. Fed by gravity, a torrent of water cascaded into the tender tank. Water towers were generally round, held 20,000 gallons or more and were made of wood, steel, concrete and even stone. In big city yards and stations, a huge central water tower serviced steam engines from multiple spouts mounted trackside.

Above:
Late afternoon light illuminates the edge of a railroad barn and wooden water tower.

184

Drinking on the Run

Toward the end of the steam era, a new technology for taking on water evolved on competing New York-Chicago mainline passenger runs. The two great eastern rivals, the New York Central and Pennsylvania Railroads, sunk track pans, or long water troughs, between the rails. Fast passenger trains traveling up to 80 mph dropped a scoop into the trough and water was forced up into the engine's tender. The procedure resulted in a spectacular spray of water that also power-washed both tender and lead cars. Although effective, track pans were expensive to build and maintain. They were not embraced by other railroads.

Above:
Steam railroads require constant maintenance. A baggage cart, ties and tools fill a back lot at WK & S Railroad in Kempton, Pennsylvania.

Below:
Gates and lights guard a crossing on the popular Strasburg Steam Railroad. Pennsylvania is dotted with steam tourist lines and museums. The old Pennsylvania Railroad was once the biggest and self proclaimed, "Standard Railroad of the World."

Steam Reliquary

Timeworn relics of the very early Steam Age—sprawling repair shops, turntable, and roundhouse—are preserved at the Roundhouse Railroad Museum in Savannah, Georgia. Built in 1835, the complex centralized the repair, maintenance, and front office headquarters for the Central of Georgia Railway. As the railroad grew, so did its shops. By the Civil War, it was one of the largest and busiest rail facilities in the South. The war and the scorched-earth rampages of Gen. William Sherman destroyed most of the South's industry, including the Central of Georgia Railway. Its Savannah complex survived, however, and continued to operate into the 20th century. After a mid-century railroad merger, the buildings were abandoned and left to ruin. Slated for the wrecking ball in the 1960s, only the intervention of civic-minded preservationists saved the massive, antebellum brick structures and their graceful arches. The half-moon roundhouse and huge engine turntable are now operational. The museum displays a fine collection of restored rolling stock and steam engines.

Above:

A soft patina of aged paint and rust adds dignity to an old passenger car awaiting restoration. The arched passageway is a vestibule taking passengers between coupled cars.

Left:

Industrial switcher, Atlantic Steel Co. No. 1, resembles a toy engine or storybook locomotive.

Opposite page:

Lime leaching from the fortress-thick walls whitewashes the ancient brick of the Savannah, Georgia roundhouse.

Overleaf:

Restored and upgraded, the old Southern Pacific yards in Sacramento are slated to become part of the already exceptional Railroad Museum of California, which is located nearby.

Acknowledgements

We greatly appreciate the generous cooperation we received from the following sites.

Baltimore and Ohio Railroad Museum, Baltimore, MD

California State Railroad Museum, Sacramento, CA

East Broad Top Railroad, Rock Hill Furnace, PA

Essex Steam Train, Valley Railroad, Essex, CT

New Hope & Ivyland Railroad, New Hope, PA

The Railroad Museum of Pennsylvania, Strasburg, PA

Railtown 1897, State Historic Park, Jamestown, CA

Roaring Camp & Big Tree Narrow-Gauge Railroad, Felton, CA

Steamtown National Historic Site, Scranton, PA

Steam Railroading Institute, Owosso, MI

Strasburg Rail Road, Strasburg, PA

Wanamaker, Kempton & Southern Railroad, Kempton, PA

Western Maryland Scenic Railroad, Cumberland, MD

So many people have kindly devoted their time and resources to help us with this project and we thank them all. However a few names should be mentioned for special thanks...
Sally Anderson, John Bush, Tom Diehl, Paul Hammond and Ryan Kunkle.

And as always, much thanks to fellow photographer and alter ego, Frank Sullivan.